PRAISES FOR DARKNESS WITHIN

"Strength- we all have it but we don't truly know its real power until we go through the unimaginable. I felt like I was right there next to Mel while reading her story. As a military spouse, my heart goes out to Mel, her late husband, and their beautiful son.

The strength it took to share her real and raw story was not easy, but her courage to do it will be able to help so many others in our community.

It's not easy reading through the heartache and pain, but it's very important to raise more awareness and help those who might be suffering silently, and to keep those pushing forward who have had to find strength they never knew they had."

- Monica Fullerton, *Owner of Spouse-ly*

"This is a powerful story of a women growing through trauma, and it is also so much more. It is an insight into the complex world of addiction, trauma and self-healing, and the impact on relationships of all involved. Melissa opens her heart and gives thoughtful pause to others to examine their own habits and behaviours when living through challenging times."

- Laura Payne-Stanley, *TED Speaker & Coach*

"I got a lot more in depth look at everything. I know several military members that suffer from some of the same issues shared in this book. Not the exact same, as no one has the same problems, but similar. Reading your book also gave me insight to the spouse's side of what they experience. It sheds a new light on everything. I hope it finds its way to the right people's hands, and they can get the proper help needed to avoid this same outcome."

- Ben L., *Army Veteran*

A SERIES OF FLASHBACKS: DARKNESS WITHIN

WRITTEN BY MELISSA ANNE

© 2021 by Melissa Anne
Cover image by Lindsay Dawn Photography

All rights reserved. No part of this publication may be reproduced, distributed, or transmitted in any form or by any means, including photocopying, recording, or other electronic or mechanical methods, without the prior written permission of the author, except in the case of brief quotations embodied in reviews and certain other noncommercial uses permitted by copyright law. If you would like permission to use any parts of the book, requests can be sent to info@melissaanne.org. Thank you.

ISBN: 978-1-7379195-9-9 (Hardcover)
ISBN: 978-1-7379195-7-5 (Paperback)
ISBN: 978-1-7379195-8-2 (Ebook)

Library of Congress Control Number: 2021919276

This book is a memoir. It reflects the author's present recollections of experiences over time. Many events have been compressed for security and personal reasons.

First printing edition 2021.

Printed in the United States of America.

Self-Published by Melissa Anne
Chandler, Arizona

melissaanne.org

ACKNOWLEDGEMENTS

I would like to thank Lindsay for the military burial photos. These weren't photos I wanted, but I knew they were needed. It's been three years at the time of writing this book and seeing those photos takes me right back.

I still remember you sharing about the yellow butterfly that left the tent that day. You didn't have to drive the hours down to help, but you did, and I'm so incredibly thankful for that. I'm thankful that I'll have them for my son when he's ready to see them himself.

Lindsay Dawn Photography, Cleveland, Ohio
Instagram: @lindsay_dawn_photography
Facebook: @lindsaydawnphotography
lindsaydawnphotography.com

To Julia, I've said it before, and I'll say it again, I hate how we were able to relate, but being able to reach out to someone in similar shoes has been a breath of fresh air. Thank you for your kind heart and your listening ear.

/ / / / /

To all who have continued to reach out, even if I haven't been able to express in words, even if you can't fully relate, I've always appreciated your words of encouragement and being reminded of who I truly am.

/ / / / /

To the casualty assistance team, I've heard the stories and seen the movies, but experiencing it firsthand was like nothing I could have imagined. You volunteer for a tough job. The grief you have to view again and again is immeasurable. Thank you for being a part of this transition, even if it's one no person desires to experience.

PREFACE

Before you begin your journey of reading my story, I want you to keep in mind that this is not like the everyday story you grab off the shelves or add to your cart. This is a series of flashbacks. While some flashbacks are in-depth, full of story, and can take up pages of your time, others might jolt you into a completely different emotion two seconds into the next scene.

As much as I wanted this book to flow in a perfect manner, *hello recovering perfectionist*, I was more determined to share my story in the most authentic manner. These stories I share had abrupt changes in emotions and unexpected twists in real life. It's an unfortunate part of trauma, and I felt it would be a disservice to avoid sharing my story in any other manner.

With that said, if the emotions are too jolting for you at times, you are wholeheartedly invited to take a pause. This book is full of lighthearted and heart-throbbing moments both side by side and spread apart. My only aim in my writing has been to share authentically with you. This writing style is a unique one, so I felt it needed to be addressed upfront.

CONTENTS

Introduction

1	/ / / / /	Our Beginning	1
2	/ / / / /	Unexpected Plans	22
3	/ / / / /	The Truth Comes Out	39
4	/ / / / /	A Child Was Born	46
5	/ / / / /	The Transition	55
6	/ / / / /	Failure	67
7	/ / / / /	A Turn for the Worst	84
8	/ / / / /	Blink of an Eye	93
9	/ / / / /	Making a House a Home	104
10	/ / / / /	Finding Forgiveness	115
11	/ / / / /	Spirituality	124
12	/ / / / /	Moving Forward	126

Closing Words

INTRODUCTION

In a letter, he* wrote to me, "*I don't know why I need this so badly. The suffering. The stress. But I know it gives me purpose and a chance to make a first-hand difference somewhere in the world. I think about Christian growing up, I hope he'll be proud of the things I've done.*"

I hope this book, read in its entirety, helps you do just that. You may not be here in this present state, but I hope sharing your challenges, ours... makes a first-hand difference to someone in this world, just like you had hoped to achieve in the world of Special Forces.

I hope this makes you proud.
Wherever you might be.

* *he = my late husband Michael. You'll get to know him later.*

Substance abusers are regularly portrayed as people with missing teeth, super skinny, and obviously not mentally there. But reality paints a very different picture.

They're the put together overachiever searching for an adrenaline kick or escape from reality. They're the war vet that never got the mental help they needed to work through things they dealt with overseas.

They're regular people seeking an escape from the outside world, or an escape from internal thoughts.

Unfortunately, with that comes the catch-22.
And sometimes, like in my story,
that catch-22 means death.

A permanent end to escapism.

My hope is that reading this book will help you find more compassion for the ways different people cope with their struggles. Not to condone what they do, but to empathize.

Maybe one day we will live in a world were people don't feel the need to escape - but, until then, the best we can do is spread love and compassion for those around us.

Often I have been asked how I was able to forgive - how I could be put through so much and still hold compassion. Hopefully in reading my story, you can gain a new perspective on forgiveness in your own life, and maybe a hint of empathy.

Melissa Anne

CHAPTER 1: OUR BEGINNING

Tennessee really did have its own shade of green, I remember thinking as I looked out the passenger side window, enjoying the fresh breeze on the way to my new duty station. As sad as I was about leaving Europe and giving up amazing snowboarding locations and out of country travel experiences, I was looking forward to the new adventures to be had at Fort Campbell.

An old friend from Germany was the one to pick me up from the airport, and seeing as I was starving from all of my travels, we chose to make a much needed pit stop on our way to base for some failed Chinese checkers at Cracker Barrel, and late breakfast. *Though I'd argue breakfast can never truly be late.*

A SERIES OF FLASHBACKS: DARKNESS WITHIN

Once settled into our bays for in processing, a few soldiers in my platoon found out that I was getting ready to turn 21. It honestly didn't mean much to me having spent the last two years in a country where I was already of legal drinking age, so I didn't really want to do anything.

Despite my feelings, the same group told me how much I *just had to come out to celebrate*, and took me out for a night of country dancing and drinking.

All I'll say about that night is that my social meter was on empty* before we even walked through the night club doors. Sleep would have been much preferred instead, and I'm pretty sure my lack of enthusiasm showed in my failed poker face.

I quickly discovered that I was far more excited about the waterfalls, hiking locations, and finding the perfect running trails than living the party scene in this new chapter of my life. *Maybe a change for the better, honestly.*

14/10 would not recommend going out with a bunch of strangers. No matter how much of a fake extrovert you can be.

A few weeks later, I was welcomed into an air defense artillery regiment as one of the new medics. The First Sergeant brought me and another female to his office to welcome us to the unit and learn more about us. As soon as he noticed my high fitness test scores, I was immediately volun-told to be one of the females on the Headquarters' team for an upcoming soldier fitness challenge against the rest of our unit.

I knew I shouldn't have been high speed coming here... I knew it would come to bite me. But there I was, competing with the guys one of my first weeks at the unit. Somehow managing to run a 6 minute mile, thanks to the competition in my veins. Something I'd never managed to do in my life, just to show I meant business and could match up with the male soldiers. Even though I thought I might puke my lungs out after completing that sprint.

From the start of my military career, I had this desire to prove I had what it took to be one of the guys. Whether that was carrying around heavy weights for a long distance, drinking too much and waking up the next morning to dominate a workout— whatever the males were doing, I wanted to prove that I was just as worthy of being on the team, of wearing the same uniform.

I wanted to prove that I was trustworthy. That even though I was a female in a male dominated workforce, I was just as capable of being by their side whenever the time came to be deployed, that I was someone they could count on as their medic.

One of my biggest goals was to not become the stereotypical female soldier: someone that couldn't keep up, that had an excuse for why they couldn't participate, that was likely to end up pregnant or married to another service member and throw their military career down the drain to become a military spouse.

I swore to myself that I wouldn't become that stereotype. I was there with a mission to help others, not for a partner or a family. Sure I wanted those things someday, but having been raised by a single mom, a self-defense mechanism of mine was this embedded prioritization of a career so I wouldn't get stuck relying on someone that likely wouldn't work out in the long run. *A belief rooted in trauma, but a belief nonetheless.* Finding a relationship or having a family just wasn't in my 5 year plan.

When I had signed up to join the military, I was torn between working towards becoming a sports medicine doctor, or being a pediatric nurse. So I knew going into the military that my priority was taking full advantage of any medical opportunities in my path to help me decide what area of medicine I wanted to end up in.

Outside of the Army, I kept myself pretty busy. I was working on exercise science and pre-nursing courses, and spent most of my spare time either studying or working out at the gym. Some of my friends that knew of my beer interests introduced me to Blackhorse Brewery and Pub in Clarksville, which soon became a favorite location to catch up at when I wasn't hiding out in my barracks room being a recluse, or off running alone on random roads and dirt trails on base.

There was just something about crossing those train tracks, getting my car parked, putting on some of my favorite tunes, and enjoying fresh air while being surrounded by trees with zero interactions, that ignited my soul. Being completely present, uncertain of how far I would actually run that evening, simply enjoying the time to clear my head on my own.

I got so used to that feeling that I convinced myself to sign up for a half marathon out in the Memphis area just two weeks in advance, despite having never ran more than six miles in my life. My mindset was, *well, I already ruck once a month where I carry a 30-40 lb pack on my back for 12 miles, what's 1.1 more miles without the added weight?* I ended up completing the race in under two hours.

Once a week in the evenings I would drive to the Austin Peay campus for a little taste of college living. I heavily felt like I was missing out on the college atmosphere, although I'd regularly joke that the Army was just like the college dorms, except we got paid to live together and party while students had to pay for a similar experience.

Attending college bible studies on their campus soon became one of my favorite parts of the week. It helped provide me with a sense of identity outside of my everyday Army lifestyle, something very much needed for service members.

For the first time in a long time, my life felt so aligned. Both personally and professionally. I was feeling my best physically, mentally, and spiritually, while also tackling all of my goals. Amidst all of my reconnecting with friends and preparing for post military plans, my artillery unit was getting ready for deployment in a few months and I was hoping to finally join in a deployment before getting out of the Army in just about a year's time.

/ / / / / future husband arrives on scene / / / / /

This guy showed up to our medic room chatting nonstop about all the things he did in SFAS. That's Special Forces Assessment and Selection for non military acronym people, or selection for short. Selection was the entry level training for anyone interested in having a career as a member of the Army Special Forces, also known as the green berets. Selection had approximately a 12% pass rate at the time, and completing the course was a pretty solid accomplishment, both mentally and physically. I could understand his excitement, but man could he not stop talking. He did have nice arms though, so I tolerated eavesdropping on the conversation from afar.

I knew that he was part of our unit, but I had never seen him before since he had been in selection when I first arrived. After that, he spent most of his time with the Special Forces Recruiting team, working out, or preparing for his next school dates. Aside from that first meeting, we rarely ran into each other unless he was at the barracks or needed something from Headquarters.

I'll never forget the first time we really talked. As I was leaving the barracks to head towards my car, he stopped me on the sidewalk just out front of the building to ask if I did Crossfit. I was instantly annoyed by his existence. There I was just trying to head out for my workout, and some guy had the nerve to strike a conversation with me when I was clearly busy.

Truthfully, I had been contemplating going to a few gyms nearby, so I uttered something like *"yea, sure,"* hoping the answer would allow me to just walk away in peace, internally pledging to never attend a Crossfit class just so I could avoid seeing him. But that didn't stop him from pursuing me, in fact it was only the beginning of his undying attempts.

/ / / / / insert *dun dun dun* for dramatic effect / / / / /

I was so over the idea of relationships, especially military ones, and was busy focusing on myself. But my answer wasn't enough. He was persistent in getting my number before I could leave for the gym. But even with my loss in avoiding his interaction that day, I still managed to blow him off for a solid two months despite his greatest efforts of connecting.

One evening after multiple failed conversations with me, he texted, *"Do you want to go for a run? I know of some good running trails that have great hills."*

He finally cracked the code to getting me to say, "yes," and so our journey began. Followed by his immediate upset reaction when he realized I had planned to take headphones.

Who enjoys talking during their runs? Did he not know that runs were designated quiet time? Despite my thoughts, I reluctantly chose to only partially listen to music so he wouldn't be a sad, pouty, little kid for the remainder of our workout.

I'm not sure why, but people always have this desire to share pains from their past with me. Even if we barely know one another. He was no different. The first time we ran together he started spilling stories about his past.

He told me about how often he moved as a kid both from his parents being military and from family instabilities. How he had dealt with physical abuse and anger issues from one of his parents in his younger years, and his brother forced him to move in with him because of the situations they were dealt. His brother even ended up pushing him to join the military to try and avoid getting him trapped in unhealthy patterns.

Michael shared about being engaged to someone in the past, and how it fell through while he was deployed. It was a typical military deployment scenario where the partner chose not to stay faithful or decided they couldn't handle the distance. Then he shared how he hadn't really had a legitimate relationship since.

His flaws included being prone to white lies, *"but mostly in an attempt to protect the other person,"* he had shared. He talked about being a medic and deploying to Afghanistan almost immediately after joining the military. Going over the number of months he spent lucky to even have MREs for a meal, and how much weight he lost on his first tour.

The difficulties of wanting to help every injured person on his team, some screaming for *"doc,"* but him knowing there was nothing that could be done. How hard it was being the one that had to choose which guys on his missions had the best chance of surviving, and only being able to treat those people.

He made it back stateside only to find his way to Nerkh Valley, Afghanistan within a year of his return.

He had just enough time to visit family, leave for his next duty station, and prepare to deploy again.

Michael talked about his experience with military behavioral health following one of his deployments, how he dealt with PTSD and had appointments in the past, but hated how it felt so he never went back after the initial session. He also didn't want a label on his record that would keep him from furthering his career.

I was a total stranger to him, and wasn't one to really open up to others right away in return, but something brought him to share these things with me. Something about me gave him enough comfort and security to open up, so I honored that experience I was given into a piece of his life.

When we started talking, I was preparing for a lot of pre-deployment training, and he was getting ready to leave Fort Campbell to start the Special Forces medic program. I knew the likelihood of this actually working out was slim to none. Because of our circumstances, I remember asking my roommate whether I should continue seeing him or not. She had the same concerns as I did, but Michael and I eventually became inseparable.

Evenings were often spent doing some type of workout in the Special Forces 5th Group gym with Chevelle playing through the speaker. Before each workout he'd jot down his own version of a Workout of the Day as if we were attending Crossfit classes and he was the coach. He always felt his best when he was able to prioritize a gym routine, so it quickly became tradition for us.

In between sets he would share his worries and the excitement he had about moving on his path towards becoming a green beret. He was so worried about failing, and what that would mean for his career goals. I would share about pre-deployment training and how much I was looking forward to being with this group overseas in Afghanistan.

If we weren't working out, we were watching tv shows, catching the latest action film in the theaters, or he was saving me from freezing in the rain or snow because I accidentally got myself locked out of my car again and was waiting for roadside assistance.*

---

*Yes, this was seriously a regular problem I dealt with and have since upgraded to a car that alerts me if I forget my keys. No more locked out problems for me.

OUR BEGINNING

/////

I spent most of my days checking off all the pre-deployment things like getting new gear and weapon qualifications in order. My unit would spend days out on the range re-qualifying our weapons that would be going overseas with us, waiting around in weather so cold that just bending a finger was miserable, let alone actually shooting targets and getting a good score.

Thankfully some of the leadership brought along venison jerky they had made, which helped shape the mood of our day in a more positive light. *We might have been frozen, but at least hangry fits wouldn't be on the horizon.*

///// road trip buses arrive on scene /////

My unit went out to Oklahoma for a few more weeks of training and mission readiness simulations. While there, I'd spend my late nights practicing mass casualty events while the air defense team did their own mock mission either in the field or in our TOC (tactical operations center) tents where communication and most of the headquarters tasks occurred.

One of the most unforgettable times there was the seemingly constant fear I had during each shift change meeting. I swore I'd accidentally fall asleep standing up, in front of all the higher up leadership, due to minimal sleep and heated tents. The only thing that really kept me awake over those few weeks was the cold wind piercing through my skin on our walks to the DFAC or our tents.

Once back from our training events, I didn't want to go anywhere anymore. Evenings that were originally spent attending Austin Peay's campus or exploring turned into simply relaxing in the barracks, music playing on Michael's computer, and introducing one another to our favorite bands or songs.

He wasn't a believer in anything other than science anyway, so he had always picked on me about going to bible studies in the first place. Saying things like *"how cute"* it was that I was a believer, in a joking semi-sarcastic manner. He had been raised Catholic, but didn't really believe in any type of spiritual world or an afterlife.

/ / / / /

We spent countless nights sobering up at the hibachi of breakfast locations, otherwise known as Waffle House… He was always so helpful with others when we were out together, and I admired that about him. He was regularly asking how he could help someone out or what they were needing.

Maybe it was the drunk feels, or maybe it was just the real Michael peeking through, but the way he would talk to people when they'd share an issue made me melt.

He would have given the shirt off his back if it benefited them in some way. It wasn't a side that was seen often, but I adored that side of him when it would show up.

/ / / / /

One evening as I listened to him play guitar, I challenged him to learn Your Hand in Mine by Explosions in the Sky, one of my all-time favorite songs, and a challenging one at that. He was so talented with the guitar that playing seemed effortless for him.

I had no idea he continued to play and learn that song over the years until I picked it for part of his funeral and his family immediately recognized it. To this day, that song still makes me think of him and the start of our relationship.

/ / / / /

We were on our way to see the zoo lights when he wanted to stop at Kmart for some things. He had me wait in the car for him, only to return surprising me with a new copy of Date Night. A movie I had mentioned I was sad that I no longer had the disc for. He must have remembered and he just happened to find it at that store.

When he got back into the car to show me, I had asked if he just happened to come across it, but he jokingly hinted about intentionally looking for the movie. It was little things like that that I admired about him.

/ / / / /

Whenever I left for training, he would joke about how he was officially experiencing what it was like to be a military spouse, *bored and alone at "home"* while I was away doing Army things. Waiting for the day I would come back again. Sending me songs like Stars by The xx. Talking on the phone with me any chance I had time for a quick chat. It was honestly kind of precious.

/ / / / /

Half of my friends would joke that he didn't exist because we never had photos together. They would joke that I made a fake account to tag someone and pretend I wasn't doing things alone. Considering how introverted I was, it wasn't too far fetched of a belief from them.

/ / / / /

We were so bad with confrontations. Our screwed-up pasts made it nearly impossible to have reasonable conversations about issues we were having. I wanted him to act a certain way in our relationship, and I rarely felt acknowledged in my concerns.

There were so many red flags from the start. He would regularly make egotistical comments about things that left me feeling like he wasn't attracted to me. As if there were changes I needed to make to match what he wanted, and I despised that.

He would joke about friends of his having kids, and showed a lot of signs that he wasn't really in a space to be in a relationship or be heading towards what I felt the point of a relationship was: to eventually have a family and a long term future together.

But for some reason I stuck it out, even though I was on the verge of breaking up with him just before leaving for deployment. I had just purchased him gifts for his birthday, made a homemade ice cream cake to celebrate and all, but I was ready to just hand him everything and cut things off for good.

In hindsight, I realize that our lack of communication and speaking up for our desires came from our own unhealed past experiences. Most of my childhood was spent being unacknowledged, or having explosive responses directed at me in the form of yelling or punched holes in walls to name a few.

I feared having to speak up for myself. I would expect the worst case: to either get completely dismissed or yelled at for speaking my truth, simply based off how my dad reacted to me as a kid. I brought that unhealed trauma to the relationship.

If my dad wasn't reacting in anger, I was used to seeing him running away from his problems. Michael on the other hand brought out an anxious and avoidant trait any time I finally managed to work up the nerve to speak up for my needs instead of dismissing them. Having his lack of correspondence, or allowing me to feel heard, only hurt me more and reaffirmed my childhood fears were right and needed for protection.

We didn't know any better. It's hard to give or show love when you've never experienced love in a healthy way. Coming from not so healthy divorced families, neither of us had a solid example of what confrontation or discussions looked like in a good relationship. As kids and as adults, we both lived emotionally defensive lives, and it showed up in more ways than one throughout our struggles.

As the years have passed and I've reflected on our start, I realized that you can only love someone as much as you're able to love yourself. And you can't be dependent on someone else for your own happiness or you will almost always be disappointed.

A relationship contains two people with different viewpoints, differing internal conflicts, sometimes opposing personalities, and it takes time to truly understand the other. It doesn't just happen overnight, and it will never be like the perfect scenes depicted in movies or books.

/ / / / /

The time came for me to deploy and for him to head to Airborne school to begin his next adventure. He was heading to Fort Benning to start in-processing that morning, and just a few days later I would be leaving with my unit for deployment.

I had worn his Special Forces Recruiting shirt to bed the night before and folded it up next to his bags when I changed for work. I remember him getting out of the shower disappointed after seeing the shirt next to his things because he wanted me to keep it as a way to remember him while we were apart, and hoped I would have snagged it.

We grabbed breakfast together and stood in the DFAC (military cafeteria) parking lot, saying what felt like a hundred goodbyes. Before leaving, he ran back to his car to grab something that had been with him in his previous deployment.

It was a black infrared flag patch that goes on the shoulder of deployment uniforms. As he handed it to me, he shared his hopes that wearing it would help keep me safe too. We struggled to finally get into our cars and head our separate ways. It felt so permanent at the time.

After he arrived at his school, he found out that he was early, so we decided to meet in Chattanooga for the day. I shouldn't have gone; I still had so much to pack and clean before my early wakeup to start deployment processing. But I went anyway.

We went to Five Guys, a place that would always be this almost inside joke between the two of us because of a very misunderstood text he received from me when we first started messaging a few months before.

While walking around the downtown area we decided to visit the aquarium, looking like little kids because we were both so excited about the penguins. Eventually ending our day date by walking around the streets of downtown, talking for a little longer. He regularly walked on the outer side of the street while we held hands; freezing, but enjoying each other's company. The subtle chivalry didn't go unnoticed.

We were sitting in the car, not wanting to leave, getting ready to have to say goodbye once again when I almost started to say, *"I love you,"* for the first time.

He beat me to it with an *"I love you too"* first. I felt like I was on cloud nine. This was the side of him that I enjoyed the most. Nothing extravagant, just simply being present. Enjoying one another's company.

I spent the drive back to my barracks hearing cheesy love songs, and I wondered what happened to my cold heart. *Did it decide to grow three sizes that day?* I was feeling all the feels now, bawling when Forever and Always by Parachute came on the station of songs— wondering what our future might hold.

I barely made it back in time to get cleared from my barracks before I was due to be in the bay for the typical Army *"hurry up and wait."*

We stayed on the phone off and on that day. I would give him updates about there being no updates, and he would reassure me that it was a typical part of the deployment experience. Our talks were the most compassionate side of him I had seen.

He shared about the plans he would like to make with me after I got home, depending on how his program went. He was so worried about passing the Special Operations Combat Medics Program. But I knew he would succeed.

After a few more conversations and numerous cat naps on cots in the hangar with my unit, it was officially time to hop on a plane for my deployment.

CHAPTER 2: UNEXPECTED PLANS

Getting settled into Bagram, I finally understood the deployment jokes. This place fed me better than any DFAC I had ever been to. I'm talking Wing Wednesdays and an iced coffee machine that felt so caffeinated it might have been a coffee brewed with coffee. The Afghan staff made sure we actually got a solid portion size of our meals, and I honestly felt guilty knowing I had other friends a few hours away living off MRE packets while I ate like royalty.

My bunkmate and I started up a routine of bringing one another breakfast or dinner because we worked opposite shifts, and it was truly the sweetest thing. She'd leave a little note on the box to start my day when she was coming off shift, and I would leave her things when she started hers.

Some of the other medics and I started an early morning run routine with a plan to run the entire airfield by the end of deployment. And let me tell you, nothing was more refreshing than going for an early morning run with the smell of gasoline, dirt, and feces filling your lungs. Whoever said Folgers was the best part of waking up must have never experienced those runs.

I was a week away from getting to start helicopter visits to the other deployment bases when my world got wrecked. I had noticed I was getting unusually tired more often. I was running to the restroom more, random nosebleeds and headaches started popping up, I was bloated, breathing was harder to do, but I chalked it all up as just my form of acclimating to a new environment. Then my period was late, but I blamed it on stress.

Another week went by feeling like this, and I finally decided to take a test. Working in the medical aid station meant I had access to a lot of supplies without needing to ask, pregnancy tests to be included. My biggest fear was getting caught by the other medics, or one of the other soldiers that were deployed with me. *Thank God our uniforms have so many pockets*, I remember thinking as I stashed a test inside and went out to the bathroom.

I was terrified to unbox a kit. Triple checking that none of the other females were coming. Panic coursing through my veins, I saw the one line that appears when you've done the test properly, then wrapped up all of the evidence like it was a crime scene, throwing my results into the trash. I didn't even wait long enough for the results to show up.

I'd tell myself things like, *"oh, it's just one line, it looks like I'm not pregnant."* As if somehow not seeing the actual results would prevent it from being true. Intuitively I knew what the answer was, I just wasn't ready to face reality. My lack of self control with the

Girl Scout cookie peanut butter Tagalongs alone should have been a dead giveaway. I literally ate two whole boxes with no remorse, in addition to having a craving for cheesy foods.

Another few days went by, and I knew it was time to get the official results. When I saw the lines on the test appear, my heart started racing. I felt so disappointed. I just became the stereotype. But at the same time, I was hopeful. I had started getting nervous that maybe it was all in my head.

After seeing the results, I went up to one of the intel offices and whispered for a friend from my unit to be my emotional support and "battle buddy" to come with me to the hospital on the other side of Bagram Airfield.

To this day I wonder what thoughts were going on in the leadership's head when I tried to run around explaining why I needed her to come with me, or why I needed to go the hospital to begin with when we had most of the needed supplies in the medic station. I wish I could remember what excuse I gave, but it was likely something about grabbing extra supplies.

I wasn't entirely sure why I picked her; I just knew I needed to have her come with me out of everyone on our day shift, and my bunk buddy worked nights, so I couldn't bring her. Plus, my friend was one of the females that I'd see in our bay at night talking to her five month old boy on video chats. Knowing she recently had a child helped me confide in her.

As we sat in the hospital cafeteria waiting on my

results, I shared my fears of the unknown, sick to my stomach with what was to come. I had waited so long to finally get on a deployment, only for this to happen. I had grown so close to the people in my bay. I was looking forward to traveling to different forward operating bases with the command team.

The deployment gym swole was calling my name before I would need to come back and start the programs for exiting out of the Army. I had plans to save up for nursing school and look into what schools I would apply to after this deployment. But instead, I was about to become a stereotype that's told of women in the military—the one I never wanted to become. I was scared to tell my family. I was scared to death to tell Michael.

Waiting at the USO to get on a phone to call him was one of the scariest moments of my life, my heart was racing, and I was on the verge of hyperventilating. I remembered the jokes he would make when a friend found out they were expecting. He was not someone looking to have a family. While waiting for my turn to use the phones, I played one bad scenario after another until it was time to actually make the call.

Part of me was waiting for him to react in a negative manner, but he took it way better than I did. In a way, he already knew what I was about to say with just my drawn out, "*sooooo...*"

That same night, he was emailing me name ideas and sorting out taking a pause in his program for a year, literally everything. All while I internally panicked, and in a way, grieved the life I thought I was going to have. The year that I had been preparing months to be a part of that was now going away.

    I was supposed to be leaving with the Chaplain to start traveling to locations in Afghanistan to do morale check-ins with the other soldiers in my unit. I was supposed to finish a deployment and come back with a nice savings while becoming a pediatric nurse. *Now what was my life about to become? What was I going to be giving up?*

    I wasn't ready to start a family.

/////

Once the military finds out about a pregnancy, you get booted out of the deployment zone pretty quick, so off to Kuwait I went. The camp in Kuwait is a lot like a beach, except you never actually make it to the ocean. Just an endless sandpit.

I felt bad for the people stuck at Camp Arifjan for months because the DFAC lacked pretty much everything. No amount of salt, pepper, or hot sauce could make the food taste better. To be honest, an MRE had better flavor than the cafeteria did.

Maybe that was just my pregnancy tastebuds speaking, but it was highly doubtful. I slept on a bunk for those few days as I prepared for my new reality and caught up with family about the coming changes.

/////

While in uniform heading back to Fort Campbell, someone offered me their first-class seat, and I felt so guilty. I didn't feel deserving of a first-class seat. *If only he knew that I only made it a month overseas. How patriotic of me. How embarrassing it was to have waited so long to finally get on a deployment only for this to be my exit. I was supposed to be the dependable one.* I felt like such a fraud. Just another female getting out for pregnancy.

But it was still a kind gesture, and it was nice to

experience it, even if just for a short connecting flight. To be honest, it ended up giving me one of the best naps I ever had on a plane.

/ / / / /

As I settled back into the barracks, Michael and I situated meeting up. We were supposed to meet in Chattanooga again like we did before deployment but he surprised me by driving a few hours out of the way and showing up at my barracks to say hi.

We checked into a hotel in Chattanooga for the weekend and experienced his favorite calzone from Mellow Mushroom our first night there. At the hotel, he was so excited about my barely noticeable baby bump. The awkward stage of pregnancy when people aren't sure if they should be congratulating you or if it's just a long term food baby.

I felt like he was honestly more excited than I was, or maybe he just did a better job hiding the stress than me. That next afternoon he watched in amazement as I devoured a burger and fries from Urban Stack in half a second as if I hadn't eaten food in ages. *Hello, pregnancy problems.*

We walked around and saw different rock climbing gyms, pretending like we lived in this little city and were finding places we would want to get involved in. Soon enough, it was time to get back to reality and situate what our lives were about to transition into.

After he got set up with a pause in his military school dates, he was preparing for a temporary location in Kansas, so I could have our son before he started his Special Forces training. I started my exiting chapter a few months earlier than my original release date from the Army, and while I was in one of my transitioning program classes, he asked me to meet him in the parking lot.

Something seemed super off about him, even just from the texts, but I took a bathroom break to see what was up. He seemed more anxious than normal, but all the off energy made sense as he handed me a box saying, *"I have something for you."*

I stared at the ring inside and immediately responded with a, *"really?"* Half in shock but half thinking, y*ou're not even going to expand on this?*

"Yea?" he replied. We went back and forth with those one word phrases until I had enough time to realize just how quick our lives were changing. *What's the worst that could happen?* A phrase I'll never think or challenge again.

But I was already pregnant with someone I barely knew, I flushed my dreams down the toilet, so at that point it really was a *"what's the worst case scenario"* moment. Not exactly the most romantic thoughts to have when you're handed an engagement ring, but alas, there we were, about to get married.

He was probably scared shitless about everything that was happening in our lives too. *"Okay..."* I said, and he went on a ramble about us meeting at the courthouse the next morning before he needed to leave to get things situated for us in Kansas.

Going on and on about how he was going to ask at the hibachi grill at dinner that night, but after getting the rings, he couldn't wait. How he wished he could have gotten me a better ring but that we could upgrade it later on. I didn't care about the ring; I was more shocked than anything. So much was happening.

I went back to class with such mixed emotions, staring at this new item on my left hand, completely missing what was going on in my class. There was this excitement that stirred up in me about this new chapter, fear of all the unknowns, grief, and a huge hint of embarrassment. I never wanted to be the person to get married shortly after meeting someone or because of a pregnancy. But here I was. Here we were, getting married the next day by some old man at the county clerk office in Clarksville.

> *What even is my life?* I remember thinking.
> *How did I go from traveling Europe, excelling in all things Army... to this? Where do I go from here?*

/////

I cried on the phone as he was sorting out places to live in our new state. "So I just have to give up all of my career goals so you can go after yours?" There I was, experiencing my first midlife crisis at the age of 21, grieving over what could have been, and worried about what was to come.

He tried to reassure me that I would eventually get to work on schooling and how this would only be temporary, but it didn't feel temporary to me at the time. It felt like I was losing a piece of myself, having to create a fake mold for the foreseeable future.

/////

While I was waiting at Fort Campbell to exit from the military, he picked out all the furniture for us, got us the apartment, and felt so proud as he showed me everything over a video call. But I couldn't help but feel like something was off about him, it wasn't something I could pinpoint at the time, he just seemed out of character.

As I attempted to analyze his behaviors more, he mentioned about our SWAT neighbor's dog and how cool it was to have them across the hall from us, *something I'd come to find out wasn't real.* He was so glad that we were living in the small college town instead of closer to the military base and couldn't wait for me to get there and see everything. He missed having me around.

/////

Within a month of living together, I wanted a divorce. I wanted to leave. I would walk around the nearby park talking to my mom on the phone about how unloved I felt. Michael would regularly joke about things like, *"when we get divorced,"* and at some point a *joke* just didn't feel like a joke anymore. I was sad because of how much it felt like he lacked compassion. How much I felt like he wasn't listening to my concerns or acknowledging the things that mattered to me despite my transparency.

It felt like all the work I was putting into playing a housewife role, while going to work and school full time, and trying to have a romantic relationship was being completely unappreciated. All of my coworkers would talk about their significant others and all the things they'd do together, the heartfelt things their spouses would do for them to spice up their marriages, but I didn't have anything good to say, so I just said nothing.

Maybe this was just marriage; maybe this was what it was like to have two people under one roof for the first time, stuck in each other's space nearly 24/7— learning how to do life together. Maybe that was our problem. We didn't understand how to communicate what we wanted in the relationship or how we individually showed our affection, and it was greatly affecting us.

I just knew I wasn't happy.

/ / / / /

We had started this tradition when we started dating of making Chef Boyardee pizzas because it was something he loved having when he was younger. He was always in charge of the dough because he was way better at it than I was, and honestly, I just really enjoyed watching him prep.

One evening he told me to look in the oven. I remember thinking it was such a strange request, but when I looked, the toppings spelled out "I heart you." *Cheesy. I know. But it truly can be the little things.*

/ / / / /

We would ebb and flow. I would tell myself, *it isn't all bad*. It was just that something always felt really off when it was bad. There were numerous nights that he wouldn't come to bed. He just wanted to spend hours on the patio. *Why wouldn't he come to bed?* I would think.

He'd mention about the dogs, but I couldn't hear anything. I'd just worry about what was wrong with him and cry myself to sleep. No amount of begging him to get some sleep would change our situation.

He wanted to sit out and watch for the cops or listen for the dogs, and eventually, I had to fall asleep. I still had work in the morning and studying for pre-nursing school, not to mention growing our child inside me was exhausting in and of itself. I was drained from the weight of it all.

/ / / / /

Being pregnant in the middle of the summer is not an ideal. So we would spend most of our Kansas summer in the pool as much as we could for quality time together. A favorite thing of ours was this silly pool game that had a few key moves: Iron lightning and Super Charge being two that I can still remember. The game was basically just an excuse to duel one another with splashes.

After numerous peer pressuring statements to try, I learned how to do a handstand underwater. He always knew how to push me to try new things and get out of my comfort zone. He even did sweet things like writing *"kick me"* in sunscreen on my back to ensure I didn't get sunburned. *Who said romance was dead?*

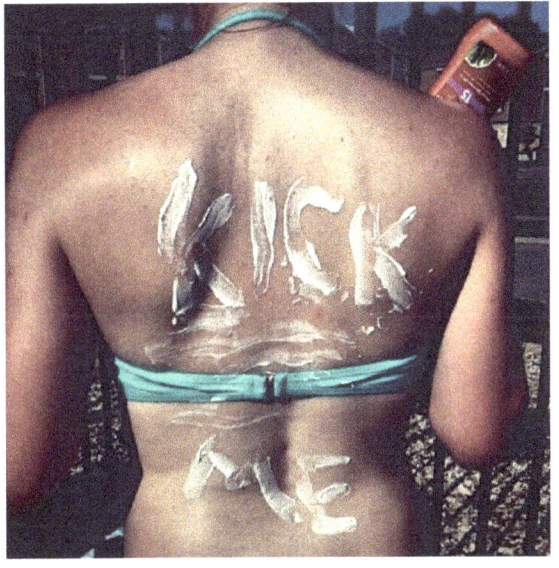

/////

Pregnancy hormones were such a wild experience. Not only did they cause me to be full of tears at times, something very much not like myself, but the changes in my body also brought on the most random onsets of nosebleeds. I remember we were lying down enjoying a movie when I started crying and laughing simultaneously out of nowhere.

I probably looked mentally unstable, but the cherry on top was when my nose started bleeding profusely as if someone just busted it in a fight, causing me to laugh even harder at the random occurrence. Thankfully I had Michael around to help get me enough tissues to cover my crime scene of a bloody nose before it got all over our blanket.

Another pregnancy experience was migraines. Michael would always make sure I took a hot shower to help calm it down, and I would come out to a hot cocoa coffee with headache medicine. To this day, I still give myself a hot shower and coffee with naproxen when I feel one coming my way, and it's because of him.

/ / / / /

I came back home for a lunch break one day, embarrassed as could be as I walked from my car to our building and saw someone perched on top of the middle roofing of our apartment complex stairwell just to the side of our patio. I hoped it was just some bored kid, but it was my husband, waiting for the SWAT to make their rounds so he could see the dogs that didn't exist.

I had to repeatedly bug him to come down and get inside. Telling him that there weren't any searches going on in our apartment complex, no police officers, no dogs, nothing would happen. He was so sure of himself that I almost started doubting my own self. Maybe we did have searches going on. Maybe there were dogs, and I just didn't see them, but everything seemed really off with him. I knew I was right, but the line was blurred.

I would then cry myself to sleep as he spent the night pacing back and forth between our front door and balcony door with his 45mm in hand, waiting for the dogs. He would look out the patio door, pause for a moment, pace back to the front door, look out the peep hole, then rinse and repeat. I wanted so badly to get the weapon from his hands, being so uncertain of what might happen if he did panic. But I also had to consider the possibility of getting shot in the attempt of disarming him. It just wasn't worth the risk of any of us getting injured in the process.

I knew it would be another couple of nights crying myself to sleep until he would be back to normal again. I often wondered what world I was bringing our child into.

Was his dad mentally unstable? Did he need to be admitted to a psych ward? Would this run in the family and be something I needed to look out for in our son? Having no idea what I got myself into, I felt so alone.

> *But who would I talk to?*
> *What would I even say?*

/////

I had to pee so bad. It was time for us to find out the gender of our child, but the ER used all the working ultrasound machines, and the other half of the machines were in repair. I wasn't allowed to pee, or we would be stuck waiting even longer. So I would just swear to Michael that I was about to pee my pants if they didn't get there sooner and did my best to stay preoccupied. He was so excited.

He had talked to everyone he worked with about how much he was hoping for a girl. I knew I wanted a boy, and I felt like it was going to be a boy. But of course, we were happy with either outcome. The moment the tech shared with us, Michael got even more excited. He started rambling on about how we could get him into wrestling camps over the summer. I was excited that I could finally pee and that I was right about expecting a boy.

CHAPTER 3: THE TRUTH COMES OUT

I knew he was lying. Every part of my body was heating up with a warning of unforeseen events. But even I didn't realize how big the lie would be. Or how it would change my life. He told me he was going out with some friends, but everything felt off before he even left our apartment. I didn't get the usual goodnight text I would expect from him if he was out, but I tried not to worry. As long as there was a text from him by no later than noon the next day, I told myself it would be okay.

The next day around noon, I received a call from a hospital over an hour away from our place letting me know that they had my husband and planned to take him off the ventilator soon to wake him up. I couldn't even eat. I called my boss, and she drove ahead of me to make sure I was okay and didn't get into an accident and end up in the hospital myself with all of the emotions coursing through my veins.

THE TRUTH COMES OUT

I got to the ICU hallway and saw the father of my child ahead of me with tubes down his throat and restraints pinning him to the hospital bed. I almost took a picture to remember that moment, as a way of reminding myself that this wasn't just a figment of my imagination, that this was really my life, but I knew it would be forever etched in my mind.

They didn't know about all of his little secrets. But now I did. On the verge of hyperventilating, I held my eight-month-old baby bump in that hallway, looked at my boss, and let her know it was okay. I thanked her for keeping me company and had her leave as I waited to get the go-ahead from the ICU staff to enter the room.

I watched as he went into fight mode, waking up and realizing he had restraints on and multiple wires and tubes attached to him. Panic-eyed but calming down a little when he saw me, and I was able to hold his hand. He just kept saying, *"I'm so sorry."*

I tried to find answers from him like, *"where is the car, where were you actually staying..."* After seeing a room card, all I could get was, *"every man has their secrets; I just needed one last fix,"* under his breath in the hospital bed. Half delusional from coming out from ventilation. I was finally able to get enough information out of him to find out where he had been staying.

I remember opening the room to his motel room, ready for the worst-case scenario. Having lived under a rock most of my life, I was prepared for every crime scene experience ever. An unmade bed from sleeping

THE TRUTH COMES OUT

with someone from the Backpage listings he was getting drugs from. Needles, or some type of mess from injecting the night before. But I wasn't able to find anything. It didn't even look like anyone had been in the room to begin with.

I even grabbed the keys to his mustang to try and find something, with no luck. Whatever he had done was done immaculately. I tried to talk to the lobby staff to see if they knew anything about what happened, but they just shared that they had helped call the ambulance for him and that was it.

After grabbing some of his belongings and checking out of the motel room, I went back to the hospital to face my reality. It all felt like such a dream. Once he was stable, the hospital staff moved us to a regular floor for another night stay.

The doctors had thankfully warned me ahead of time that he would still have some of the drug effects in his system. So back to hallucinations he went, only this time it was him imagining people on the rooftop of the next building through our window.

I tried my best to sleep on the reclining chair for the night as I quietly cried myself to sleep once more, if I even slept that night. He just continued to pace for the rest of the night, periodically checked on me to ask if I was okay, then he was back to watching the imaginary rooftop people for the remainder of the night.

When we were up the next day, the hospital staff let him sneak a quick dip of chewing tobacco outside while we talked. He shared about how he had planned on writing me a letter and explaining it all to me, how this was his last time, but then he panicked and didn't want to end up in jail.

How he would rather die and have me and our son receive something than end up in prison for having illegal substances. I still didn't know what to do or think; all I wanted to do was cry. He just kept sharing how much he loved our soon-to-be son and me, how we meant the world to him. I wasn't sure what to believe.

He had a huge canker sore in his mouth from being intubated, so they prescribed him medication to help with the pain. I remember being so disappointed by all of it. There was no genuine recommendation for therapy. They even prescribed him an opioid for the pain, after knowing he just overdosed.

I was beyond upset with the healthcare system from that point on. Maybe they were just so accustomed to drug abuse that they didn't blink an eye anymore. But how quickly they were ready just to let him go. No speaking with a therapist or anything for psych. Essentially just a, *"try not to take a fatal amount next time bud,"* and sent on their way back home.

No one was phased. No one. And I get that I'd spent most of my life under a rock, but for someone to be okay with risking their career, their family... for a fix? That wasn't something I could just brush over. But I didn't have time to truly process any of it because my baby shower was a few days later, and I had a shadow of myself to portray. I was about to have a child. I didn't have the mental capacity to figure out where to go from there.

Thanks to a social worker, I was able to get us a civilian counseling appointment at a local coffee shop, but Michael didn't want to attend. Unfortunately, I also knew before even asking that he wouldn't be attending. He was very clear on his experience with behavioral health in the military and was set on not going again. It wasn't worth him risking not going through the Special Forces program or ruining his career.

So I had to show up alone and apologize for the wasted time. I too decided to brush it under the rug for the time being. Hoping he would seek help on his own terms, and went back to my 9 to 5 job, pre-nursing school, and growing my photography business.

He put up the best façade for everyone around following that incident. Acting like nothing was wrong, like our lives didn't just have a huge situation happen. But then again, so did I. My family would be in town for my baby shower, and I'd act as if nothing happened. Like my life was perfect, and I couldn't wait to bring my child into this family. But every piece of me knew I was lying to myself and to everyone around me. So who was really lying?

/ / / / /

After my baby shower, Michael was undeniably the responsible one of the two of us. He was the one to baby-fy my mom car by figuring out how to attach a car seat base to my Chevy Equinox. He was the one to put together the entire crib, the one constantly getting on me about making sure I had my "ready" bag packed for whenever I went into labor.

I just did what my procrastinating self did best and put everything off. He even helped paint my toenails when I randomly had a pregnancy nesting desire to paint them, and my baby bump was too big to reach.

It wasn't until I was already experiencing pre-labor contractions a few days before that I finally decided it was time to pack a bag.

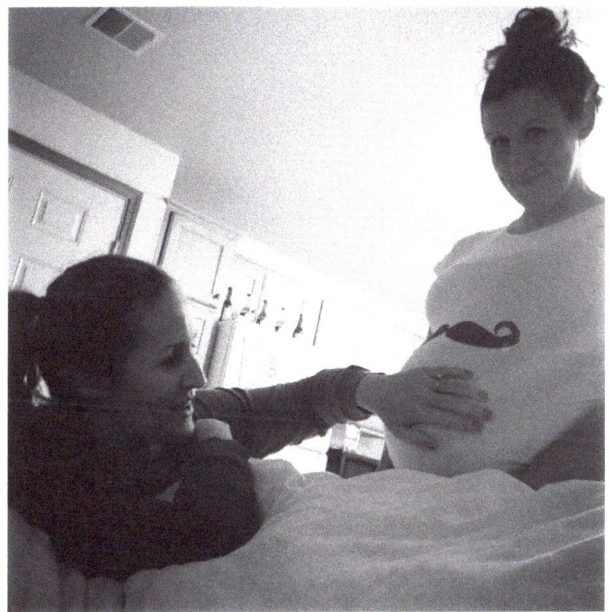

My Mom and Me, October 2014

Maternity Photo with Michael

CHAPTER 4: A CHILD WAS BORN

I had spent an entire weekend having pre-labor contractions, but they weren't close enough to be admitted into the hospital. Michael and I called in from work that Monday just in case I went into labor, and he had a plan in mind for our entire day.

///// enter get this child out Olympics /////

He was running around the military base looking to borrow a medicine ball from some of the people he knew so I could try bouncing to induce the labor. He made me the most disgusting, spiciest hamburger helper I had ever tried.

We walked up and down the massive hill near our apartment that overlooked all of Manhattan, Kansas. Michael made sure I did as many things in the books that were supposed to induce labor, and I had finally listened to him about packing my ready bag that he had been hinting to me about for the last month. Monday, just before midnight, I was admitted to the hospital.

Throughout my pregnancy, Michael and I would pretend to have conversations with Christian. We would speak to each other as if we were him with this Blues Clues meets Mickey Mouse type of peppy humming sound to pretend like he was interacting with us. When I went into labor, it made everything feel so much more real. Our son would no longer be this pretend voice, but a real baby with real noises, and real-life experiences. Even though we had prepared for this for months, it was an entirely different feeling going into it officially.

Michael knew that I wanted a natural birth, so we planned to have music playing on his iPod home and my essential oil diffuser of peppermint and lavender in the hopes of bringing calming energy to the room. Anything I needed, he was ready to help with.

I was so drained that my eyes stayed closed almost the entire time I was in labor from having maybe six total hours of sleep the last two days leading up to my true contractions. Michael held the shower handle over my back and adjusted the heat however I needed off and on for hours. I remember being so thankful that the hospital staff finally let me take breaks from lying in bed to move and be under the heat.

All I remembered was how much pressure I was feeling on my back. I'm not even sure that I really existed that entire time. I just remember Michael telling me what a great job I was doing and how well I was tolerating the increased intensity in contractions based on the readings, while holding my hand throughout the entire experience.

Throughout the nonexistence I was feeling during my labor process, I do remember the random compliments from the labor and delivery staff about how great my room smelled. And the comment one of my nurses made when the song "Honey, it's Alright" by Gregory Alan Isakov came on for probably the hundredth time, saying something along the lines of, *"yea yea, we get it. But it's not morning anymore."*

It was only at that moment that Michael and I realized how unobservant we had been to the background noise we set up and finally changed the album from The Weatherman to something more shuffled.

When we got to the point in the labor where it was full-blown delivery time, Michael was so excited to help grab Christian with the doctors. I remember being so worried about letting him be that up close and personal for the sake of our romantic relationship in the future. Still, Michael's medical side was super excited to be a part of the birthing process, so I let him.

Getting to cut the cord was one of his highlight moments, next to holding our son for the first time. I remember feeling like the worst mom in the history of moms when Christian officially arrived. I was so drained that I didn't even want to hold him. I was afraid I would drop him if I did and seeing just how fragile he was made me so worried I would hurt him somehow.

The good mom persona came out really quick though

when they had to take him to another room for testing, and I started crying. I just wanted to have my baby nearby us.

Michael wasn't one to share his feelings much. I would get subtle things to show he cared, though. Before leaving for field exercises, he would write on a piece of paper that he loved me and would tuck in my teddy bear where he'd sleep. At one point, he gave me flowers with a card that said how our son and I meant the world to him, and about an ice cream treat waiting in the freezer after a wedding I photographed. But the words he wrote while I was sleeping after delivery are some of the sweetest words I had ever seen written by him, especially publicly:

> *"To the most amazing and brave woman I know; Melissa you went through roughly 31 hours of total labor without a single medication to induce contractions or relieve pain. The whole time, the only thought I could process was "please, how can I make you feel better." The intense battle that you fought through was one not many could say they won. You are my role model, my idol, my angel, my best friend, and my wife. I will never have to worry about our new son, Christian, because he will always have you. Rest up, be proud. I love you."*

We had been transferred to the outpatient room lying in two separate hospital beds with our son in between us in the hospital bassinet. I remember Michael cried in the room that night. He just kept looking at this kid we created together, my strength, and the beauty of parenthood coming over him.

Seeing this kid we used to have pretend voices for now in our arms. I rarely saw that emotional side of him, so I couldn't help but admire how beautiful it was to catch some of his vulnerability. Whether it was my hormones carrying the room or what have you, it was a sight to see.

He was always so concerned, so nurturing, so worried about anything and everything, so in awe of this precious child we created. Looking back, I can see where our son gets all his anxious worries and protectiveness from. Michael was so thankful for our family and for having our little boy with us.

Back at home, we would take turns with baby watch. He would stay up playing Destiny on the Playstation, and I would rest. He'd get me if Christian needed fed and he would do the diaper changes, then I would take dayshift.

/ / / / /

ONCE HE WAS 6 WEEKS OLD, I GOT INTO A CRAZY SCHEDULE:

6:00am - Drop Christian off at daycare

6:30am - Gym workout

7:30am - Shower and off to work

Midday - Take breaks to breast pump and study

5:30pm - Michael and I would get him from daycare after work

6:00pm - Spend the evening studying some more for my online classes, taking exams, cooking, cleaning

Late night - Nursing Christian off and on

I don't even think I could get four hours of sleep a night those first few months, and Michael wasn't able to help much because Christian was so picky about only wanting his mom half the time. He was still always so concerned if anything was even the slightest bit off with our son. I would try to justify that everything was fine, and Michael was always two steps away from taking him to the hospital *"just in case."*

/ / / / /

When either of us would run errands, we would send one another these silly text messages acting as if we were on some type of medieval quest. We overdramatized what we were doing by sharing about side quests or dragons along specific roads causing traffic, and using renaissance age wording for everything.

If we weren't in the renaissance era we were pretending to be Englishmen and slightly hoped Christian's first words would have some type of accent because of our constant shenanigans.

A CHILD WAS BORN

/ / / / /

Christian was maybe five months old when Michael and I talked about his future during one of our many walks together. Discussing whether or not we would get him a car when he turned sixteen*, college funds, the list went on. Michael was always the planner of the two of us.

*Christian, if you're reading this... your dad said you get a car. Not a new one, but you get one.

///// his mustang leaves my work /////

Michael left for airborne school, for real this time, and I remember him coming by my work to get one last farewell. It was weird to think how fast the time went by and that it was already almost time for us to pack up our things and start our new life in North Carolina for his Special Forces Program.

I held down the fort at home with our son while he made the "take two" of his training. During our time in Kansas I had started building a photography portfolio, and wanted to make it my full time gig when we got to North Carolina. I started networking with wedding vendors in our new state and making lists of wedding venues to visit so I could be on the right steps when we arrived.

I was still working on pre-nursing courses, but it was finally time to take a pause until I knew we would be staying somewhere for a while and I could actually complete a full nursing program, so photography was taking centerstage instead.

CHAPTER 5: THE TRANSITION

It was officially time for us to start our new adventure. It was time for Michael to go after what he had put on hold for an entire year so he could be present for the pregnancy and delivery, and some time with our son before life became nonexistent for him. North Carolina bound we were.

We got settled into our house on base so Michael could be closer to the school and not deal with gate traffic. Truthfully I was pretty nervous about making military friends on post. *Were the stereotype stories true? Would the spouses only talk about their kids and their husbands? Was there any hope for me? Did I have to truly become a housewife now?*

The instructors with the Special Warfare Center and School informed the families on day one that we might as well treat this training as if they were deployed... for the next two years. So I kept myself busy, as I always did. While Michael was in school, I was out driving around and growing relationships with event venues, wedding vendors, and attempting to make friends.

I had even tried to join a military spouse only get-together in our neighborhood. As a former service member, it went very much not okay, as I quickly learned of the stereotypes I thought were only rumors. Thankfully, within a month, I made some solid military spouse friends who had lives outside of their spouses, where I could truly relate and had common ground. Things were starting to come together.

/ / / / / prepare for family fitness day / / / / /

Michael had a fancy "special operations approved only" rucksack that he wanted to test out, so we packed up the car, grabbed the stroller, and went to the track on post for a family workout. He didn't think I still had it in me to keep a good ruck march time, so naturally, I had to prove him wrong:

> *"When your husband dares you to do a ⅔ mile lap around the track with his 45lb ruck in under 9 minutes and you do it in under 7... #stillgotit #2yrhiatus"*

We finished doing laps around the track and headed for the multi-use pull-up bars to complete our second workout when he asked for my phone so he could look up a workout idea. I remember thinking how nice it was to spend some quality time together despite his busy schedule.

But the mood quickly changed when he saw my internet tab open discussing drug abuse and related actions as the current browser topic. He didn't say a word, just handed my phone back with the open tab in view and an obvious disappointment realizing that I was still digging into this topic. He was ready to go home, and we didn't talk the rest of the night.

After a lighthearted evening, I was disappointed to see how quickly it crumbled. We had never worked past what happened in Kansas. And things weren't okay, no matter how busy we both made ourselves. Trust was still lost, and this program wasn't helping us work towards building a new foundation. No amount of pushing the situation under the rug was going to work for me.

There were so many questions I still had that he wouldn't answer. He still wasn't willing to seek mental health care or any form of counseling with me, so I was left searching for answers alone. I was creating a narrative of my own from the minimal answers I had from him about his actions. While simultaneously putting a smile on my face and hoping maybe one day I would wake up with trust magically restored. But we tried.

We would take beach trips with Christian. I tried to do the housewife things like hanging up decorations around the house, failing DIY Pinterest projects for our backyard, and even spending time getting our front yard cleaned up for attempted gardening after Michael mentioned how much he liked our neighbor's yards. I continuously acted like everything was fine.

But it wasn't; I wasn't. There were so many times I would let my thoughts drive me mad, not knowing if I could even trust that he was truly studying. My worries were pushed even more after speaking with a pastor at a church. The pastor narrated the cycle of addiction and essentially let me know it would be a lost cause, that it was just a matter of time before things would spiral again.

But I wouldn't talk to Michael about it; I couldn't. He would just get upset that we were still hung up on what happened and how he had hoped our move to Fort Bragg could be a fresh start. Instead, I would attempt to share about my day of wedding vendor networking, and he would barely pretend to be interested, while I at least tried to share in the excitement for his stories about new things happening in his program.

We focused most of our time on Christian and his recent changes while spending zero time on ourselves, and completely ignoring our current struggles. There was no passion between us, and I was constantly on edge waiting for the next let down.

I realize now that I couldn't be mad about him not

sharing his struggles with me in detail, because I wasn't willing to acknow-ledge my own within myself at the time. Just like he tried to keep himself too busy to accept his demons, I was doing the same.

He didn't know that there were so many times Christian would be laying on me, and I would have suicidal ideations. Thinking of ways to just no longer exist. Thoughts like, what if he just cut off my breathing on accident and I just let him. Ideas that made me feel so sad for even having them cross my path. Deep down, I knew I could never do that to my son, but nonetheless the ideations were there, and they were strong. I was tired.

Looking back, I probably suffered from postpartum depression but just never talked about it because I still hadn't even recovered from what had happened less than a year before. I just knew I didn't care to be here anymore, and no one else knew about it. Once again, I faced the world with a smile and pretended like I was living my happiest life.

/////

THE TRANSITION

They say a picture is worth a thousand words.
But what about perception?

You might look at this photo and see the growth of a child. A curious kid.

Most times I see that too.

Other times I flashback. I'm instantly back in a house where Christian took his first steps. The house where I was growing a wedding photography business while raising a toddler almost single-handedly.

THE TRANSITION

I held distrust. I hadn't really processed all that had happened not even a year prior. I had brushed under a rug all the lies I had been fed. The cheating just to get drugs. The overdose. Somewhere in the back of my mind wondering when the next "fix" would be.

Would he survive this time?

There were so many times I didn't even want to exist. Why? What was the purpose? What life was I even bringing my child into.

A bunch of broken people unwilling to get help?
To confront their demons.

These thoughts would run through me as I went about my day making sure a child stayed alive, keeping a house clean, making food, networking with local businesses, trying to make new friends in this new state I was trying to make a home.

Will he ever seek help? How long will it be before I find out next time? Have I reached out to this company to take photos and blog about their venue? Does Christian need a diaper change?

When did I eat last?

But then he'd come home and I would act like everything was fine. It was f i n e.

/ / / / /

But it wasn't fine, and I knew that the moment I threw that plate full of fresh ham and eggs into the sink after he left to study that Saturday morning instead of sitting to have a quick breakfast with us beforehand. Watching as the ceramic plate shattered and food flew everywhere. It was not fine. And we probably wouldn't ever be fine at the rate we were going.

/ / / / /

We were planning to have a vow renewal. Something deep down I knew probably wasn't a good idea considering our circumstances, but I never got a chance to wear a wedding dress or get professional photos done of us as a couple, and I already felt so cheated in all of the "first" experiences a normal couple typically has. I hadn't received a true proposal, and got married mid pregnancy by an old man at a courthouse. I needed to portray a happy marriage self to the world. I needed to pretend like something in our relationship wasn't a complete shit storm.

I had a friend on the phone with me as I was about to look into flights for her to come out and be one of our few guests when I came across his emails tab unintentionally left open. My distrusting curiosity chose to look through and see what he had been up to. Numerous sent emails showed up for Craigslist Backpage listings from our time in Kansas with him asking for potential no strings attached hookups followed by email after email of him asking if they had access to different drugs. He wrote things like, *"I promise I'm legit. I'll prove it,"* while he asked for the drugs by street names that I had to lookup.

As my whole body heated up and my hands began to shake, I immediately told my friend I would call her back later. *This was the last straw,* or so I told myself, as I packed up a few things for Christian and I to stay the night with an old military friend of mine and her husband. To say I was livid would be understated.

But Michael managed to talk me off the ledge of moving back home, stating how the emails were from the past and we already went over this, how he wasn't doing that anymore. I stayed, but remained on even higher alert from then on out.

/ / / / /

All of my hard work networking with local wedding vendors was finally paying off. I started to book my first weddings, my gym routine was super solid, I was growing awesome friendships with military spouses in the area that were also entrepreneurs.

Christian was about to have his first birthday, and I

was once again keeping myself busy as Michael stayed preoccupied with his schooling. I think my subconscious thought process was, *if I stay busy enough, maybe I won't realize just how much my marriage is destroying my life.*

We made it as far as Christian's first birthday before another issue came up. His phone was left unlocked and forgotten at home after a lunch break. By some act of God, I saw what I didn't want to see, call after call to more Backpage women lasting only seconds each time to maybe a minute. And after yet another failed attempt at talking with him and a counselor about our situation, I decided I was going to pack up our things and move back home, absolutely heartbroken and tired of the façade I kept putting on.

Michael didn't take the decision of me leaving well. I watched as he threw my stuff into trash bags and tossed them in the living room. Holding onto our son as he walked around the house telling him things like, *"don't ever get married Christian. It'll just end up like this. No matter how much you try to fix things."*

Fearing him lashing out and getting physical in his upset state, a fear rooted from my childhood, not at all from my marriage, I texted a friend to have the Military Police called for me. I knew if they were called he would be forced to stay in the barracks for at least 24 to 72 hours. If I was going to actually leave this time, I had to make the moves to get myself out in peace.

A look of absolute betrayal showed on his face as he

looked through the living room window and saw a military police vehicle pull up in front of our house asking him to come with them. It was hands down the most bold move I had made in our marriage, but it was a necessary one.

The military police took him away, let me know how much time I had to myself, and I proceeded to take that time to get a Uhaul rented, and thankfully found a military spouse friend to help me get the larger items into the trailer. The same friend that had just been over with her husband for my son's first birthday party. Even with her, I only shared the smallest truth to the reason for me leaving. I would just tell everyone he cheated and that was it. While I wanted to let people into the storm that wrecked my world, I didn't want to ruin his career.

I'll never forget that friend sharing a statement made by her husband when she shared the news about us separating, *"I mean this respectfully, but how could he have her as his wife and still feel the desire to cheat? They seemed so happy at the birthday."* with her immediate agreement. It was only then that I realized how much of a fake front I had maintained for all this time.

CHAPTER 6: FAILURE

    Not even a full day of driving down, I fell into a full-blown anxiety attack on a dead-end road in the middle of nowhere near someone's farm. The Google maps hadn't updated about a road closure, and I was stuck figuring out how to fifty point turn my SUV and Uhaul trailer on a one and a half lane road without tipping over into the mudslides just off the road, with my child in the backseat sleeping. I remember honking the horn so many times, banging on the steering wheel while bawling my eyes out, hyperventilating, upset that I was all alone to do this.

    How did my life get to this point? Where did I go wrong? What did I fail to ignore and why did I have to be the one to go through these lessons?

Once I settled into a place in Arizona, I cried filling out our divorce papers. This was never what I wanted. I never wanted this to be the result. All I wanted was a normal relationship. A normal marriage. A normal family. Whatever normal might be.

Sure my partner and I would have our problems, and we could work through them, but not to this degree. Without even a touch of willingness to get the help needed. I had so many unanswered questions with just one *"I don't know"* after another from him. Or *"If I knew, I would tell you."* but no answer was ever enough to help gain back trust. It felt long gone. Hating myself for how obsessed I was with checking his call logs on our account.

I remember internally freaking out when I decided to call a number I had seen pop up on his call log, and it ended up being a girl he had just slept with. She shared about everything that happened and how he wasn't even the only person she slept with that day. How she was off and on with another military guy but he was busy so she decided to hook up with Michael. We had been gone for barely a week and he was already on dating apps. If I needed a sign that I made the right choice, that was it.

I built up a routine for myself while staying with family. Go to school, take care of the child, get child to bed, get a workout in, shower, listen to worship or instrumentals for hours, and bawl my eyes out on the couch about my situation.

For weeks I would pray for him to get the help he

needed. I would pray that he would find some form of faith, some type of hope required for change. Not for me, but for himself. For his relationship with our son.

I would sit there thinking about how much I would rather spend my entire life single than go through that ever again. But that it would all be worth it if he could find the change and faith needed. Eventually, I stopped praying about him.

I moved in with a friend and continued to build my photography business on the side, with school as my main focus. At the time I had completing my pre-nursing courses and was on the waitlist to begin nursing school. But I needed the extra money while I was growing my business, so I transitioned to a marketing degree instead so I could still get money from using my GI Bill.

Michael would schedule a weekly video chat with our son, worked through his program, and I focused on my own life. It was so strange seeing two people become complete strangers.

We had to wait a few months to begin the actual divorce process, but I decided to start getting on dating apps around the six month mark of being back in Arizona when I officially filed for our divorce. Deleting the apps within days due to my dis-interest in over half of the population. Deciding to focus on myself once more. It was better that way anyway.

/ / / / /

AROUND EASTER OF THAT NEXT YEAR, HE WROTE ME THIS LETTER:

"I know I hurt you in the worst way someone ever could. Nothing will change that... One thing I can tell you is there is no pain worse than the pain you bring upon yourself. It's a pain that creeps behind you when you walk down the street, it lies beside you when you go to sleep, it leads you down horrible directions when you let it get too close. I have done horrible things, and they always come back to remind me that I can never undo them."

"I should have wrote this letter a long time ago."

"I've never been the best at anything, but I have always found ways to become better. I can be a better person. I need to be. For me. For you. For our son."

"I don't want a divorce."

/ / / / /

He sent me flowers, and a balloon for Christian, in an attempt to show he could change and start doing the little things.

We flew out to spend a week in North Carolina so Christian could see his dad while I was on my summer break and we spent the day in Raleigh enjoying a craft beer and cider after letting Christian wander around the Marbles Kid Museum for half the day.

We picked out a cute outfit for him from one of the local boutiques and walked around the city park. I could tell Michael wanted us to be able to work things out, but I wasn't sure. I knew there was so much lack of trust still, but I could see ways he was slowly growing, and I wanted to believe the best.

If we were to get back together, I was going to need time. I knew he was getting involved in a church, volunteering in his limited free time, and trying to communicate with me more. Deep down I knew I wanted us to have a successful marriage.

I was so back and forth. I wanted so badly to work on things, but I was also terrified. I was scared of going back through the situations I was still recovering from.

What if it was worse next time? Was the chance worth the failure? Was the marriage even capable of being saved?

Christian and I went back to living our Arizona life, and Michael continued his schooling. I would send him periodic articles about marriage and ways to make it a success. I even sent a new wedding band Etsy listing with some joke about if we wanted to have a fresh start while deciding shortly after that I wasn't ready to work on this, that I wanted to move forward with the divorce instead. I was so scared of getting heartbroken again.

A little while later, he wrote:
You sent me this message a week and a half ago.
I know we can make our marriage work.
Even if you don't think so right now.

Winter of 2016, that same year, I flew out to Ohio with our son so they could spend time together again. Michael's family is from there, so we would tried to visit when we could. At the time we were both seeing other people. We weren't officially divorced, we had chosen to hold off until the new year to officially sign for it, but we weren't together.

I was only really there because Christian couldn't fly alone, and truthfully I think I had my own anxious attachments about being away from him. So I sat unsociable on the other end of the couch or hid in the bedroom the first day or two. But Michael knew the stupid ways to get me to talk or give him attention.

One evening, he started reading out loud from a list of the cheesiest dad jokes he could find on his phone until I eventually acknowledged his existence. We ended up grabbing a six-pack of Not Your Father's Root Beer from the store and sat on a futon in the basement talking about life for hours.

He eventually started talking about the ways he wanted to be a better husband, and how it didn't matter that we had both been dating other people during our separation. How I was still the mother of his child and he would always choose me over anyone else. That he still loved me and always would.

During our time in Ohio, he started asking about things going on with me better. We even held hands while he or I drove, something we had never done before. There were subtle acts I had started seeing from him that were things I wanted from him before and was now finally getting. It was starting to give me hope.

I remember after playing a game of Cards Against Humanity with his family, my sister-in-law asked if we would officially be staying sisters, and me sharing the news that we had decided we would be staying together so the answer was, yes.

We didn't tell hardly anyone about getting back together, but we made plans for our son and I to move back out to work on things. Michael flew out to help us move our things back from Arizona to North Carolina, and we honestly had a perfect time. I introduced him to In-n-Out's secret menu, he experienced what my version of "almost packed" meant, and we spent some quality time with my mom and step-dad, introducing them to Cards Against Humanity as well, where I learned a whole new side to my mom that I will not be able to unsee, but she definitely won.

Michael even met some of my closest friends for a double date, and they really enjoyed his company. I remember him sharing how he wasn't surprised I came back to Arizona and how much better the area was than where we had lived at Fort Bragg, but truthfully I enjoyed the East Coast more. On our drive back to North Carolina, we would share comedy podcasts to listen to along the way and periodically talked on the phone for updates.

Things were onto a good start, but he was heading into some of his final field exercises like Small Unit Tactics (SUT) and Survival Evasion Resistance and Escape (SERE) training, and I quickly realized how unrealistic it was for us to make this work with his career path.

To get through everything I went through with the minimal time he would have available was going to take a lot on both parts. I was doing my best to be a stay-at-home mom, but I feared getting hurt again. I continued to grow work relations with wedding vendors in the Fayetteville / Raleigh area.

At that point, I had changed my college major to marketing since I wasn't sure when I could start a nursing program with Michael's schooling. I reconnected with military spouse friends I made my first move living there, got involved in the YMCA, and continued attending the church services.

Christian and I had a schedule going again, but I was still filled with anxiety and fear of if Michael and I could genuinely make this relationship work when I knew he would be gone all the time in this career. *Could he really change? How would I know if it was genuine or not? Could I handle another heartbreak?*

/ / / / /

FAILURE

30 April 2017:
"Melissa, as I lay here in the dirt soaked in sweat and dust, all I can think about is talking to you. Today marks the beginning of week 5 and it feels like week 6 can't come soon enough. It's been a rough time, and I'm worried I will be spending another 6 weeks here. It's hard to stomach the thought that I have to be open to the idea that I have to tell you and Christian that I failed. For now, I'd just like to think about spending time at home. One thing that replays in my mind constantly is all the ways I've done you wrong, but out here I feel like I'm paying for it ten-fold. I hope I'm in your thoughts, you're in mine."

/ / / / /

    I was considering leaving again. All of my insecurities were pulling back up to the surface and I worried about if I made the wrong choice in coming back. Maybe this wasn't such a good idea. I didn't have close friends or family. I was essentially a single mom. He had already said no to counseling in the past.
    Maybe it would be better for me to start fresh without all of this emotional baggage and unhealed problems in our relationship. Maybe it'd be better for Christian if his parents weren't together, even though I so desperately wanted things to work out.

/ / / / /

2 May 2017:
"I volunteered to carry the 2-10 today. It's about 100lbs of equipment and ammo. I never thought I'd see the day I thought a 60lb ruck felt light. I should go. I just wanted to talk. I keep dozing off while I write this. I love you."

6 May 2017:
"I really don't want to come home and tell you I failed. I don't want to have to needlessly be out of contact from you guys again… When I write the letters it feels like I'm having a conversation with you… I see you in less than a week. I love you."

/ / / / /

Your Hand in Mine played on my shuffle, and it almost brought me to tears. I thought of the better times we had. I wanted so badly to have a healthy relationship, a healthy marriage. How badly I wished I could just erase the past and start fresh.

I wanted Christian to have a better example of what a good relationship looked like, so he knew the standard as he got older. But I was so heartbroken and torn. I had become so cold, so numb, to the relationship.

Nothing had really changed, no counseling, no willingness to pause in the program to work on things, I was just attempting to brush things off and hope it didn't happen again. The only real change was that he started getting involved in church, attending bible studies, and volunteering. But our relationship had so much work to do to feel like we reached a decent place of security.

/ / / / /

10 May 2017:
"I just got the word, I'm moving forward. Most likely, I will be right back here on Monday for SERE-C... Just wanted to write and share the good news. I love you."

/ / / / /

While he was in the field, I took a road trip from North Carolina to Maine and back to clear my head. *Yes, I went on a 15-hour drive for a few days' stay, followed by another 15-hour drive back...* to clear my head. During that drive, I decided it was best to separate again. I had no idea about the letters until after making the decision. I just knew I wasn't ready, and I didn't feel we had time to make things work.

Mother's Day was just before he went back to the field for SERE school and a friend of mine took me out for a bottomless mimosas brunch date to celebrate me being a mom.

I came back to our apartment to see Michael had colored a card with Christian and wrote *"Happy Mother's Day"* for me with our son's name on it. He had even talked to Christian about how pretty mommy looked, and it all just made me really torn.

These little things were what I wanted, what I had wanted these last few years. But I was scared it wasn't authentic, or if it'd last.

/ / / / /

WHEN HE LEFT FOR SERE SCHOOL, HE LEFT ME THIS NOTE:

"During SUT, I started appreciating everything I took for granted. I prayed, a lot. I learned to cope with the things I cannot control. Maybe that's why I'm not upset over you leaving. Me asking you to stay would be like you asking me to leave the Q Course. You need to go just as much as I need to finish the pipeline.

I've accepted the fact that I'm choosing a lifestyle that doesn't breed healthy families. I don't know why I need this so badly. The suffering. The stress. But I know it gives me purpose and a chance to make a first-hand difference somewhere in the world. I think about Christian growing up, I hope he'll be proud of the things I've done.

I'm going to be fine. I've got plenty of things keeping me distracted. The funny thing is, that's my biggest problem. Six weeks of misery gave me a lot of clarity. I wish I had a chance to tell you how much I thought about you. I had a lot of stories. Maybe when I come back from SERE I will be even more humbled than I am right now. I hope my spiritual connection with God continues to grow as I continue to put myself through these horrible conditions. I hope I find a part of me that I've been searching for while out there starving, being beaten and 'tortured.' It's such a good feeling when you can look in the mirror and say you learned something about yourself.

Take care of yourself while I'm gone. I still love you. Always will, even when all I want to do is hate you."

/////

When he came back from SERE school he handed me some of the letters he had written me, but held back from others. I only knew about them because I snooped and ended up taking a picture of them with my phone and went for a walk, bawling while reading them all.

/////

27 May 2017
"I have made it to day 2 of our FTX. I haven't really ate anything in 3 days. We have been making lists of foods to eat after we get out of here next weekend. I hope you read the letter I left you. I'm crossing my fingers you're

giving everything some thought. Just know that I'm exhausted and starving but I'm thinking of you. I should be home Friday from SERE. Although I've got you on my mind, all I can long for is food. 3 days of absolutely no food has me weak and distracted. I try to think about home, I get food instead. I try to think about you, I get food instead. I try to think about Christian, I get food instead. I'm going to be so grateful for the simple things in life when I'm done with this course. Just wanted you to know I still love you."

28 May 2017

"The countdown has definitely started on coming home. The days seem to drag on forever with no food. I talked about you with a friend today. I wish you weren't leaving. I want so badly to work on our marriage. All this pain and suffering that I've put myself through, I did it with you pushing me along. I would tell myself things like, "I can't go home to Melissa as a quitter or a failure" I wish you knew how much of a difference you make in my day. If I could just kiss you one more time, maybe you'd know how much I mean it. Anyways, I love you Melissa. I'll be home later this week and I hope we can talk about this. I want to be more passionate and a better man for you. See you soon."

/ / / / /

FAILURE

These words, these things, were all things I had been praying about years ago. I wanted this to work so badly. But I knew Michael wasn't going to have time to work on himself the way I needed him to, or so I told myself at the time.

How it was easy for him to say these things while in the worst of worst situations, but wondering what would happen once he was back in the real world. Maybe I was too hardened and afraid of crumbling had it happened again. Afraid I'd be unable to get back up the next time around.

I felt ripped into two pieces. The one that saw this as an answer to prayers long ago prayed for, and another of distrust. Disbelief. Maybe I didn't have the strong faith I thought I had. I knew for a fact that I let too many other voices cloud my decisions. Voices that only knew a portion of the story, but provided my requested two cents. My friends and family all meant well, but maybe I shouldn't have relied so heavily on their opinions.

Looking back, I should have just stayed silent. I should have allowed myself time to think without others clouding me, without just acting defensively and running away. *Something I've always been the best at doing.* But I didn't. I was scared to be let down and hurt again, so we separated once more.

We went to church a few more times. He helped me sell my things, and he went on a boy's beach trip with our son before I moved back to Arizona... again. On better terms, or at the very least a mutual understanding of our needs, but it still broke my heart wondering if I was acting out of fear rather than trust. Wondering how many voices I let cloud my judgement.

If I had truly listened to myself, or if I listened to the opinions of others more. It was too good to be true for me to believe he could be changing into the person I had hoped he could become over these last few years. Or was it?

What if I was the problem this time? What if I jumped the gun? But I already made the decision. I have to leave now, right?

I shouldn't have let so many opinions get to me. I should have just kept the relationship to myself to sort out. I wanted to stay, but I was afraid. Afraid of having genuine happiness in a relation-ship, something I had never truly experienced. I didn't want to get hurt again either.

I may never know what truly made me decide to move, but the fact is that I moved, regardless of where my heart was.

CHAPTER 7: A TURN FOR THE WORST

We moved back home to Arizona, but we were able to meet with Michael in Flagstaff at the start of October while he was doing medical sergeant training. It was his last specialized training for Special Forces before beginning the final phase, followed by language school.

He was able to spend two days with our son climbing Humphreys Peak. While he and his team were out working on their fitness, I came across a craft beer festival happening that weekend and enjoyed the fresh Fall atmosphere that the valley rarely offers while trying out local brews.

I remember making sure I looked extra nice the day he got to pick up Christian to remind him that I still looked good, that mama still got it. Even though I wore heels and he hated when I did that since I was already an inch taller than him without shoes.

Petty me aside, there were so many things I wish I would have told him. How proud I was of how far he had come, or how happy I was that he was almost finished with the program. But I didn't.

I just kept the conversation about Christian and left the rest to silence. I wished I would have at least hugged him before he left. I hoped maybe things could change for us after he finished his schooling and found out where his Special Forces Group would be, but only time would tell.

By late October, "something came up," and he was no longer in the program, only he didn't tell me what happened or that he was no longer moving forward. I was back in North Carolina for a weekend to photograph a wedding and initially planned to stay in our old apartment while he went to the field exercise, but he never went. He told me he wouldn't be joining his group for the Phase V of Robin Sage training and wasn't sure when he would be joining the next group.

Every question I had for him was answered with a vague response back, and the same internal intuitive flames came up inside me about his answers. I tried not to worry about it, hoping maybe he'd come forward about it when we saw each other.

I meant to meet with him to grab some of Christian and my things from our old apartment before my flight, but with regular updates back in Arizona about my Grandma that was in the hospital waiting to pass away from cancer, something I had avoided truly accepting for over a year, and me catching up with old friends, I completely spaced it and didn't have enough time to swing by before heading back to Arizona.

Michael and I never saw one another that trip, even though I really wanted to see him and see his in-person responses to my questions. A huge piece of me just knew he must have gotten into trouble. Nothing else would have made sense for why he wasn't moving forward with something he worked so hard to achieve the past few years. He had to have used again.

It would be another year and a few months before the military would provide that answer for me. Because he never did, and likely never would have.

///// enter hospital scene /////

A TURN FOR THE WORST

A few days after landing back in Arizona, I was saying my goodbyes to my grandmother in the hospital, the kindest woman.

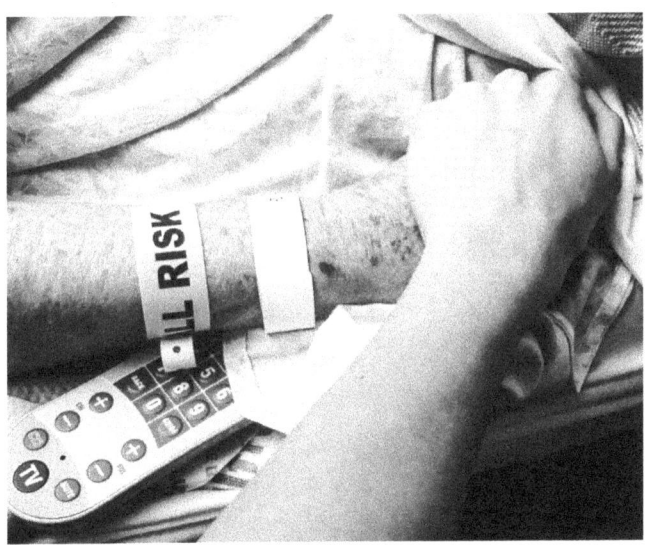

A TURN FOR THE WORST

/ / / / /

Michael and I didn't talk much anymore. He got pretty quiet after our Flagstaff visit and the missed meet-up in mid-October. We didn't say much, aside from periodic texts about him getting into school classes, considering leaving the program, or a random text about a show we used to watch. It all just felt so off.

I knew a lot of it was from my own lack of responsiveness, but I had started to become so upset about his lack of a relationship with our son that I wanted almost nothing to do with him. Michael had stopped asking to talk to him for some time, and I was so angry about it all. So disappointed.

I stopped letting him see updates on my social media in hopes that maybe he would reach out to check in on Christian, but he didn't. Instead, he just made jokes from time to time about me doing his statistics homework, some fitness things, and that was about it.

Towards the end of the year, he recommended a book to me that felt super unlike his character. It was a book called "With: Reimagining the Way You Relate to God" by Skye Jethani. I knew he volunteered at a church periodically and joined in bible studies when he had a moment, but to have him recommend a book about connecting with God felt so foreign to me from the Michael I first met just a few short years ago. The one that made jokes about me being a part of a Bible study, him only being a believer in science, it was interesting, to say the least, seeing this change happening in him.

January of 2018 was the last time he spoke to our son, for maybe ten minutes if that, and my heart was broken.

How could someone want nothing to do with their child? I remember thinking. How could someone just go about their life for months like it's nothing? How could someone deliberately choose not to experience all of these first few year milestones?

Like he just had this new life now, and our son wasn't a part of it. I was livid for months on end. Incredibly disappointed but not willing to speak up about the situation because I wanted Michael to be the one to initiate time with his own son.

He got more involved with a church group with kayaking trips, camping, hiking, and off-roading. It seemed like he was working through some improvements. Even though he didn't really exist at all in our lives, I hoped he was healing. I hoped he was finding what he was in search for. I hoped he was still going after his SF career and not giving up, even though he hinted at pursuing nursing instead.

He randomly congratulated me for officially earning my bachelor's degree, but we didn't really talk outside of that. He had slowly become a stranger. But then again, I wasn't sharing anything either. I wasn't asking him about his life, and he wasn't asking about mine. The year went on...

On paper, I seemed pieced together. I lived in the cutest Downtown Phoenix apartment, hosted semi-monthly get-togethers with friends, booked business trips, and all the feel-goods. But real life behind closed doors me was spiraling into a deep depression again. Truthfully, I don't think the postpartum depression that I failed to acknowledge ever went away, it just cascaded into a chronic state, and other things were piling on top of it. Financially I was upside down. I was working myself to the bone with no break in sight, just a hope and prayer I covered the next month's bills in time. I was tired.

I no longer wanted to be here anymore. The suicidal ideations were making their way back to me. Thoughts would come to mind of how I could leave this place with the least amount of trauma placed on my child. *Could he stay with family? What could I do?*

I remember thinking how nice it would be for Michael to finally have our son for a little while so I could just breathe for once. I was mentally, physically, and emotionally tapped out.

Over the summer, my nursing school waitlist finally got back in touch with me, and I was preparing to start that in the Fall. After a few years of not seeing the success I wanted in my photography business, I was completely burnt out and wanted something that would be more stable. I had planned on downsizing my rental space to afford to breathe a little, and I was going to step away from all the hats that being an entrepreneur had and focus solely on being a caregiver and attending school.

As I was preparing things for the semester so Christian could be in daycare, I came across those letters Michael had written me a year prior. I remember sitting on the floor in tears as I reread his words, thinking that maybe we could start over from scratch after he finished his schooling.

Maybe once his group station was situated, I could get a place nearby so our son could continue a relationship with his dad, and we could rebuild a foundation. I knew he had talked about possibly getting out, but he was so vague with me about everything. From his previous schedule, I knew he would be able to graduate any time that summer, but little did I know that my answer to moving forward was going to be a 'no' soon. The loudest 'no' I'd ever received.

Michael texted me a few days later while I was out having dinner with Christian during one of our monsoon power outages downtown. He was messaging me about a Netflix account our son must have made. He shared a photo, and I can't remember what the account name was.

I kind of wish I still had the old messages to see for sure, but I made some joke about it probably being Christian's imaginary friend. Deep down, I wanted to call Michael. I had this urge to video chat with him while eating dinner, but I didn't. We finished our food and went back to the apartment.

I had hoped he would respond, but he never texted back, and I figured maybe he went to bed. I wanted so badly to share with him the thoughts I had been having after coming across those letters again with fresh eyes, but maybe we could talk another day when it wasn't so late for him.

CHAPTER 8: BLINK OF AN EYE

I woke up to a missed call from somewhere in North Carolina. I almost answered it, but I couldn't think of anyone I didn't already have a number saved. A few hours later, I got the news from my sister-in-law.

/ / / / /

What do you mean gone? Did he run away? I remember thinking as she shared. *We just texted last night. Where'd he go? How can he be gone, gone?* He was just talking about Christian's account, and I made some dumb joke. There's no way he's gone. Am I really going to be in this alone? Like completely alone now?

Would anything have changed if I had decided to video call him last night like I felt called to do? Would this still be our life now? Could that call have stopped this from happening? How is this reality? There's no way this is my reality.

I didn't even want to be here anymore. My business was not succeeding. I was financially failing. The idea of continuing to be a mother and somehow staying afloat was causing me to drown. Most days lately had been spent thinking about what medications I might have that I could use to overdose, or if I could bring myself to the bathtub scenarios seen in films.

What would be the easiest on others? What would be the quickest and least painful option? No, what about Christian?

Why did Michael have to be the one to leave? How come he got to be the selfish one? When do I get a break? Now I have to raise our child even more alone than I was before. What am I supposed to do now? I should have been the one to leave. He was the one with a steady career. The one that actually knew where he was heading in life, unlike me and my mess of an existence.

/ / / / /

Sitting against the bathroom door, trying not to hyperventilate. Chest tightening. More tears covering my face than I'd felt in years. A three-year-old completely unaware of how his life just changed drastically in minutes was having a fit on the other side of the door. Mad because I was losing my shit and unable to face anything more than this empty bathroom and a whirlwind of emotions all at once. Everything was a blur.

How could someone feel numb and so many feelings all at once? Like I was no longer in this body, but could still feel every emotion pulsating through my veins. How could something not feel real yet cause so much wreckage?

What if. What if I had video chatted him like
I felt called to do that same night he left for good.

I had to stop allowing myself to *what if*.
No amount of that would change the past.

BLINK OF AN EYE

/ / / / / enter airport setting / / / / /

I did my best to keep it together, to appear strong. I told Christian we were picking Daddy up from the airport, but that we wouldn't be able to see him. That it would be different this time. It wasn't until we were standing on the tarmac and Christian asked where Daddy was, as they rolled out my failing marriage on a conveyor belt that I nearly dropped to the floor in tears.

I watched as the scene I'd only experienced in military films or photos was happening to me in real time. As someone that didn't even want to be a military spouse became a member of the Gold Star family, and an honorary member of the Young Widows Club.

*I had no idea these photos even existed until finalizing this book

As I was escorted back to the car by the most wonderful officer I ever had the opportunity of working alongside, Christian threw a continuous fit about not seeing Daddy. He wanted to see Daddy, and all I could do was utter back an, *"I know babe. I do too. But we can't see him the same way anymore. He's not here anymore."* It was time to bring Michael back to his hometown.

/ / / / /

All I wanted to do was sleep and never see that flag or a person in uniform again. Police vehicles chauffeured us to and from the tarmac in a ridiculous convoy of motorcyclists and regular vehicles, showing their support. Fire Trucks parked on the side of the small town roads with flags hung up in honor.

Stranger after stranger held flags and waved them as we passed. Hats were off and held at the heart in respect. I wondered what he'd be thinking. If he were in a grave, he'd probably be rolling over in it, but maybe he'd be honored. I didn't know. But all I could feel was fatigue and sadness for the triggering long-term effects I knew those items would now hold in my mind.

/ / / / /

I lost my shit at the Fayetteville airport kiosk. The keys were still in the rental car right outside the door. I was trying to balance holding a child, a car seat, and all of our luggage with these two new flags I didn't even want in the first place.

I lost it so bad that I cussed out my child. Cussed out myself. Hyperventilated. Started bawling. Left half my stuff on the floor. And asked to have my flight changed to the next day because I couldn't breathe, and I was tired of being in the scene I didn't even mean to create.

Nothing even happened in the airport. No one was rude. Absolutely nothing bad happened. But my tipping point had been reached and everything went crashing down with it. I wanted to apologize. I hope I did. But I was completely checked out, and I only wanted one thing.

After days of running around to different courthouses and attorney offices to get the legal approval to access our old apartment for his things, I just couldn't leave without seeing it one last time. I needed to see the way he left it before the movers came to grab everything. Partially in hopes of closure, I needed to experience how he was living before leaving us.

An old friend tagged along with me for emotional support while another volunteered to keep Christian at her house with her girls while I did a walkthrough.

I finally walked into the apartment, the one he moved into when we first separated. The one I lived in for a few months when we tried to work on things again. I pictured him in the kitchen where he took his last breath. There were no answers for me about how he died yet, only speculations. I would have to wait another few months to a year before finding out the details of his death.

He was never a spiritual person, but the book he recommended for me around the holidays a few months before was sitting on the breakfast bar, and a bible in the living room. Dip can placed next to his PlayStation controller. Photos of our sweet baby on the coffee table.

There was the window where our sweet boy would eat food on his Ikea kid's table and watch the cars driving by, where he would bring up "daddy's car" when Michael would get home from work, fingerprints always coating the glass. The spot where he helped Christian write my Mother's Day card.

My snowboard and a storage box were sitting in the hallway, the items I was supposed to take home with me in the Fall of the previous year. The second bedroom still had all of Christian's things in it almost exactly like we left it, and there were tons of photos of the two of them and of Christian sitting in Michael's room along my old desk.

I could feel his sadness. I could feel the cloud that followed him around in that place. The cloud that followed him for months. He was always really good at putting up a front. No wonder. We mirrored each other in that way. But I knew he had demons, and I could feel a handful of them still lingering as I walked around. It broke my heart.

Whatever happened. Whatever he was going through, those last months specifically… if it was even half of what I felt in that apartment, a lot made sense.

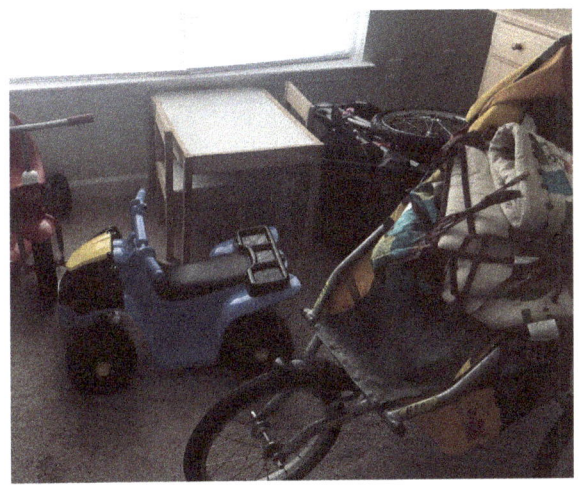

/ / / / /

I didn't know what to tell him. Where his dad went. What did I even believe? It was only after Michael died that I truly questioned my faith and if there was anything past this world.

Maybe it was just all for nothing. Sure I told him his daddy was in heaven, but was he? Did heaven even exist? Was there even a happy ending to this hell-hole-filled experience called Earth? I sure hoped so, but I was numb to it all.

/ / / / /

Deep down, I envied him. Regularly I envied him to some varying degree. Why did he get to leave? Why did he get to be the selfish one? He was heading down a path he'd always dreamt of while I struggled to stay afloat in all areas of my life. Not know-ing what path to choose—so consumed by the thoughts racing through my mind.

The ones telling me how much of a failure I was, to just give it up already. That I would never see success. I would never reach the financial goals I was working so hard towards. How terrible of a mother I was because I could barely give my son attention or help him grow the way I wanted to.

That I wasn't ever going to have the love relationship or family I always dreamt of. The one I wrote about in journals as a child. How it was too late for any of it.

I didn't even know which thoughts were mine and which were the voice of another living in my mind rent-free. What I did know was that I was tired—tired of struggling—tired of feeling like a failure. Like everyone thought they knew me, but really most didn't have a clue. How easy it can be to give the world a façade.

A half-smile to light the world while inside is turmoil. A loving conversation while breaking down internally. Stuck somewhere between wanting to save the world and wanting to be done with this world. With its chaos and confusion. With the heartbreak and breakdowns. Simply wanting to just feel at home. Whatever home was supposed to feel like.

CHAPTER 9: MAKING A HOUSE A HOME

> *"Before you go, just be sure this is what you want. If it is, I pray that you can get Christian settled in a home that he can finally stay in. I know you'll be okay, just give our son a home he can stay in."*

That was the last request I had from Michael in a letter he wrote to me, and I wanted to so badly. Not just for our son, but for my own self as well. I craved stability too. Growing up as the kid that moved every other year wrecked my ability to ever truly know what it meant to settle down. What it meant to have a home that I could stay in. And I wasn't even a military kid.

Everything in my life had always felt temporary. The location, the friendships, family, even my marriage. It often felt like I was given things for a short season and then they'd be gone, as if they never existed. I often joke that I suffer with abandoned puppy syndrome: this expectation from past experiences that I'll get left behind, stuck fighting for my own survival, unable to trust.

Learning to ride with the wind, afraid of what it might mean to grow genuine connections. Just waiting for the next betrayal. So in an effort to avoid being abandoned, I chose to constantly be on the run. Never truly growing roots, never settling down, never allowing others to grow close, or the opposite. It was the best defense mechanism I could think of, along with expected letdown.

But what if I didn't allow for self-sabotage? What would it even be like to settle down and grow roots? To genuinely feel like a place felt like home to me. What was home?

What he was asking of me was a lot. Maybe not for the person that grew up with the same people most of their life, but for me... I didn't think it was possible, but I was still determined to try.

As I was waiting in North Carolina for paperwork to get taken care of so the military could move Michael's things, I hopped on Zillow, and a few pages in, I thought I came across it. I ended up driving all the way back to Ohio for a quick visit just to see what I swore up and down was the one. The forever home.

The house was in the perfect price range for me. It had plenty of room for growing up in, an open living room and kitchen area for hosting get-togethers. The sun set behind the gorgeous acre and a half of a backyard, an area that would be perfect for all the cousins to spend time at with Christian.

It was even down to the details of being minutes

from a local coffee shop and brewery, something unheard of for a small town. I swore it was going to be the home, our home. The one Michael would be proud of... I mean it even had the most beautiful blue accents inside, my favorite color. How could it not be the home?

///// the first home buying experience /////

It was bumpy, but we made it happen. I got the forever home, and I started furnishing it perfectly. But it felt like one roadblock after another came up. A few bridges seemed to have burnt before I even had a chance to build them. Family on Michael's side that told me things like, *"you and Christian are family, we're here if you ever need anything"* at the funeral that summer quickly disappeared within just a few months of us moving in.

Others didn't seem to truly understand the mental and physical toll of trauma and grief. How despite coming to a small town and trying to create a forever home, I wasn't ready to start growing new friendships right away.

I needed time to be a recluse, because I genuinely only had the energy to stain a deck and be available for my son. I wasn't ready to truly hang out and act like all was well yet. I didn't have the energy to interact with others. I needed time to just process all that happened in my life in a blink of an eye.

I wasn't ready to fake a smile, and I sure as hell didn't have the energy to explain my life circumstances to random strangers, let alone anyone for that matter. I needed time.

/ / / / /

I sat there in the taco bell drive-thru for breakfast one morning with tears filling my eyes. It was random things that would spark a memory and make me cry, like passing the movie theater, an ambulance, or seeing an American flag. I hoped eventually I wouldn't feel these emotional triggers so intensely.

/ / / / /

When I was finally ready to start interacting, I almost immediately regretted it. The depths I would go to avoid telling our story. To avoid one more, *I'm so sorry for your loss* statement. I would dig a ditch of uncomfortable confusion before finally admitting our life situation that brought us to this small town. Most people eventually found out, and it was less of an ordeal, but the first little while was a time I wanted to avoid for as long as possible.

It was always hard to hold new conversations because I never wanted to be the buzz kill-mood buster, whatever words you'd prefer. It was hard to go from *"yea this beer is great. I love this coffee"* to *"by the way, my kid's dad died. Yea.. I'm a widow. That's why I moved here."*

There was never a fun way to go about the discussion, and I quickly wanted to move past it once I finally shared our story.

/ / / / /

The ideations came back. I would regularly find myself driving with numerous *"what if I just..."* thoughts along my drives home or out somewhere. *What if I verged off the road? How fast would I need to go? Would it be able to kill us both?*

I would quickly change my mind, but almost solely because of the likelihood of either me dying and my son being left alone, him dying and me being left alone, us ending up in critical condition and surviving but living a rough life, or someone else getting hurt on accident. I couldn't intentionally let any of that happen.

/ / / / /

I started flying out of state for weddings and taking Christian on some fun trips. Over the course of a year, I explored Boston, Connecticut, Maine, Tennessee, Florida, Canada, and even went on a Marvel Disney Cruise. Professionally I was heading on a great path too. Overall I was feeling really good except for sleeping half the time to avoid dealing with my emotions.

I was also drinking unhealthily, practically living off pizza, and barely taking time to exercise despite having a home gym—all things I once took really good care of in my life, but managed to put on the back burner.

/ / / / /

If I was going to make this place my forever home, I knew there were some key things I wanted to have to truly make it my own little retreat, and I was offered the help to make it happen. But that intuitive heat moved across my body again, and I soon discovered more false promises.

Some of Michael's family that supposedly *had our backs* ran away with tens of thousands of dollars and nothing to show for it. I started diving back into living defensively because I realized I had started to let my guard down too much and I was tired of people just saying things to make me feel good, then never stick to their word. I was tired of being used and feeling like an idiot.

Grief was overpowering me, realizing I was once again living for everyone else but myself. I was disappointed by how much I had been led astray when I was just trying to do the right things for my son— frustrated by the busy excuse and lack of action by so many I had moved here to grow a connection with. I got tired of throwing a pity party for myself. I was tired of waiting on others to come around and find time to spend with us.

If I wanted to make this house a home, I knew that I had to start doing things right, with or without additional family. When I first moved into the house, I remember falling in love with all the hills because it meant I would have plenty of trail runs to go on around the town, so I started running again. Along those runs, I would befriend the local farmhouse dogs while freezing my butt off in the winter weather.

On the verge of getting on antidepressants, I decided I would at least make a genuine effort to change my current living situations first. I didn't like the idea of putting a bandaid on my feelings, but tired of my depression and missing true community; I knew something needed to change.

It was just after Veteran's Day when I saw a video from WeDefy Foundation about veterans adjusting to civilian life and how the foundation helped through jiu-jitsu. I knew I needed to bring the old me back too, so I joined the closest jiu-jitsu program near my house and was instantly hooked. *No pun intended.*

My new routine became hitting the road around 5 am to make the 6 am class, feeding my kid on the way to pre-k, then working on either traveling to the other towns to network with wedding vendors or editing and designing for clients. Things felt like they were finally going smoothly for the two of us.

I was getting a routine down, growing relationships with people I regularly saw at the brewery and coffee shop. My wedding photography clients were absolutely amazing, and I was booking weddings for venues I had on my dream list. I even gained some wonderful design clients, but I still felt incredibly drained and empty outside of those interactions.

I loved the connections I was making, I loved the house, the potential, but I couldn't help but feel like something wasn't right. Despite so many good things going on, I was still sleeping a lot. I still felt like I wasn't in my purpose, like something was missing, and this house was too big for just me and my son.

I got left with so many household responsibilities, and it was a lot for a single parent with minimal support to take on all alone.

As much as I wanted to make this house a home like Michael wanted, this wasn't it. As much as I had grown wonderful connections and created a little family out of the friends I made, I needed something else. I felt lost.

I had started everything I wanted to. I found baby success in all of the things I started, but they didn't feel right. They didn't feel like the "impact" I wanted to make. I hadn't created the life-saving feel of an impact I was feeling drawn towards deep down.

Sure I was great at wedding photography and loved connecting with the couples and the guests. I heavily valued having beautiful photography to capture moments in time, but to some degree I think my military side was coming out far too often and felt like so much of what I was pursuing was superficial and first worldly.

I knew it was time to leave and find career success elsewhere. But where? I felt like I was failing. Like I couldn't keep to anything, and I was so disappointed in myself.

As if bearing the weight of both parental roles as just one person while singlehandedly pushing through grief wasn't enough. Somehow being the caregiver, breadwinner, house cleaner, meal supplier, keeping in shape, trying to be social, etc. wasn't enough. I had to wear every single one of those hats while getting maybe four hours of sleep if I was lucky. Something needed to change.

/////

I cried in my bed with my child lying next to me. I was once again thinking about the different ways I could go away from this world. How tired I was. I just didn't want to be here anymore. I was bawling, looking at my sweet child in the bed next to me.

I knew I wouldn't. I couldn't. What life would that bring for my son? But the thoughts brought me to sobbing tears regardless of if I would do it. I was so tired of the thoughts.

/////

I loved the simplicity of country living, being able to look out the windows from my bed and see all the stars in the sky. I enjoyed how quiet our home was. You could see the lightning bugs making all the trees and bushes look like they were sparkling under the night sky. They would always remind me of being with Michael in our Kansas apartment.

How funny he thought it was that I didn't know what the twinkling lights in the bushes were until he explained it to me from our balcony one night.

I explained to him that I didn't even know lightning bugs were actually real when he shared how he would catch them as a kid.

While I wanted to make this place our forever home, I couldn't. I was so thankful for the experiences it provided us: a chance to slow down, see what things mattered the most to me, and see that I could accomplish the things I wanted to accomplish To realize that sometimes, a lot of the time, things aren't like we initially envisioned they'd be. But it was time to go back to Arizona like I always did when times were hard and I needed a reset. With great sadness, I sold the *forever* home.

///// procrastination for packing commences /////

Arizona has always been my anchor, in a way. The place I could always count on to help me when I needed redirection. While I was devastated about leaving this house, I knew I needed to go back to my own form of roots and figure things out.

So much had changed in my life, and I just kept myself so busy. It wasn't until the COVID-19 pandemic and everything having to close down that I realized I wasn't where I wanted to be. While I knew I was helping others, it wasn't at the level I wanted to be at, and I was tired of wearing all of the solo-preneur hats in a field I wasn't even interested in. I was ready to go back home to friends and family and figure it out again.

CHAPTER 10: FINDING FORGIVENESS

> *"I was never addicted to one thing; I was addicted to filling a void within myself with things other than my own love"*
> - Yung Pueblo

After moving back to Arizona, I started a Masters of Social Work (MSW) program. I hadn't realized how much of my career oriented "helper" goals went away and were replaced with my marriage, having my son, and becoming a widow. I wanted to pursue so many career paths over the years, but they always had to do with helping others towards having a better future.

After everything that had happened in my marriage, and my life in general, I knew I wanted to do what I could to help others in similar footsteps. If there was a way to help military members, their families, or veterans in either of our shoes, I wanted to work towards that. Within a few short months, the triggers, flashbacks, and depressive, anxiety-ridden episodes returned. I wasn't ready.

I was only a few months into the social work program, but I had chosen to focus on substance abuse and trauma in veterans for my topic of choice to do research on throughout the program, and it started to weigh heavily on my mental state.

While attempting to get research papers completed for my classes, I would be reading midline from medical studies I was using as a resource, and be mentally brought back to the hospital when he had tubes connected to him after the overdose.

I would snap back to reality and start writing my papers only to be brought back to the day I opened the autopsy report and was given the official answer I had waited over a year for. Mailed straight to my doorstep and opened in a parking lot so I could avoid having to react to it in front of my son.

///// blurring into Michael's secret life /////

I would envision the play by play from the criminal investigation that was included with his thorough autopsy report. The events that occurred the night of his death. Large black boxes covering anything the police or military felt needed excluded from public eye, but keeping great description of everything else.

There I'd be trying to type up my research papers at the final count down because I couldn't stay in the present. I could have reread the same sentence five times, but that sixth time it would bring me to his apartment. Envisioning his conversations with another soldier as they injected steroids, then him searching: cocaine and baking soda, huffing glue, seven days of cocaine, and prostitutes. Ending the night with him dead on the kitchen floor.

There were missed calls and text messages left on his phone from unsaved numbers asking if he wanted to pick up "gurl," a possible code for cocaine. Lab results would soon reveal fatal levels of cocaine toxicity, alongside fentanyl levels 4x over the lethal dose, a drug commonly used for lacing street batches, and a common culprit for unintentional overdoses.

He would then be found dead on arrival the next day after a failure to arrive for duty, discovered by apartment staff and military personnel. Around that same time was when I would be receiving the calls from the apartment staff and my former sister-in-law about the news that he was gone.

///// focus back into Mel's life /////

While in the program, I had also decided I would be a gestational carrier for this couple at the same time. For those that don't know, in a perfect world, a gestational carrier essentially hosts a couple's embryo and carries the child to full term, has a healthy labor, then delivers the couple a healthy child that they get to hold and take home as their family. A lot more goes into it, and a lot of emotions, but that's the most basic of what the concept is.

In true Mel fashion, I overcommitted and once again put everyone's needs above my own, and I finally cracked. I went from holding a 4.0 to barely being able to focus on assignments. The idea of going through a pregnancy and reliving flashbacks of my first pregnancy was destroying me mentally. But the fear of having to let someone down was holding me back from getting out of this hole.

I knew I wanted to help people, but working through the social work program and the carrier process made me realize how much I hadn't actually healed yet. In my program, I chose to focus on researching topics relating to trauma, substance abuse, and the military population. After months of getting into a better mental state, I quickly found myself resorting to old coping mechanisms that entailed of mostly sleeping my day away.

Something had to change, so I said no, and I ugly cried. I finally put up boundaries, a little late, but nonetheless put up, and I ugly cried giving updates. Not only did I decide to pause the MSW program, but I broke the heartbreaking news to the couple of where my mental state was at. I chose myself, and it still broke my heart, but I knew it needed to be done for my own sanity and to be a good mom to my own child.

During my hiatus from the program, I started diving back into old interests of mine. After getting out of the military, I received a military scholarship to become a personal trainer through ACE Fitness, so I decided to start studying that.

I invested in a health coaching program, and I decided it was finally time to write this book. I wasn't entirely sure where any of it would lead, but I've always trusted that my intuition doesn't lead me astray when I choose to actively listen. But like with any major changes in my life, I knew I needed to go for a drive to clear my head and situate what direction my life was truly heading from here on out, so off to Colorado* I drove.

To get to Colorado from the valley of Arizona, you have to take a trip up through Northern Arizona. It's one of my favorite drives because Northern Arizona always reminds me of a combination of Colorado and North Carolina. The trees are so tall, the air is fresh, and it's just an overall beautiful road to drive on when in need of serious mind clearing. This drive hit a little differently for me, though.

I hadn't really thought about it before, but this was the same trip I had taken nearly four years before when Michael and I met up over a long weekend during his military training for him to see our son. I started realizing things in his shoes for a moment. How depressed I would have been after seeing my child for all of two days, knowing I wasn't really sure when the next time would be.

*No... I don't believe in short road trips. Colorado is a day trip. It takes a day, and it's a trip.

Michael saw his son and wife, as complicated as we were, at the start of October. By late October, he had ruined his dream career, the same career he wrote note after note to me about how he didn't want to come home a failure. How he didn't want to tell me he didn't make it. It was no wonder he never told me about what was happening.

No wonder it never came to light that he was getting out of the military. He wanted our son and me to be proud of him. Instead of sharing the truth of his situation, he told me a lightened version, and I spent literal years so mad at him after he died. He knew he was chaptering out of the military, and he never bothered to tell me. I had been so livid with him about the entire last year of his life.

But that drive helped clear my mind. Something about those trees brought in the recollection. The negative talk he probably had, his own disappointments, his *"what now"* mentality.

Learning about addiction, trauma, and brain chemistry between the two, a lot of what I had to deal with in our relationship made sense. I had always struggled because I felt like everyone had these wonderful stories about Michael, and here I was with the darkness and triggers.

But we both messed up in our own ways. I didn't have the right questions to ask, and I filled in the blanks with my own stories of what happened that were probably worse than whatever truly did happen. He was coping in the only way he knew best, and didn't want to ruin his chances of reaching his goals in the process. Thinking he could work through it on his own instead, much like me.

If I were to do it again, I would learn more about imperfect-ion. Learn more about love languages. Learn more about unmet expectations and how they don't immediately mean failure. I would remind myself that it takes time to learn another person, especially when two people come from brokenness and unhealed lives. It will never be the fairytale life, but it takes effort to focus on the good instead of pinpointing all of the bad. If you're too focused on the bad, you overlook all of the good that's right in front of you but blindly missed.

I don't regret separating. If anything, I feel us separating was needed for some of Michael's growth. But I do think marriage and relationships are so often treated as replaceable goods. When you choose to be with someone for life, you're choosing their ups and downs and allowing them to see your flaws too.

Choosing to be with someone means working through difficult chapters together, even if it's in separation for a period of time. And it's not to say people don't go through legitimate trauma and abuse and need to get out of dangerous situations and never return. I'm not brushing over those by any means.

But maybe we throw words like narcissist and gaslighting around a little too much. Maybe we need to look at the way we are mirrors of those in our lives and get a better understanding of how or what lesson the situation is trying to teach us. I feel it could help us heal in a better way if we can begin seeing ourselves in those around us.

Thinking things like, *how can I relate to these actions in my own way?* Or, *in what way have I been this person to others?*

When I look back at that final year, I've had to find my own forgiveness as well. When I find myself in the *"how would I have done things differently"* mentality, I have to remind myself that I don't know what could have, would have, should have happened.

What if this same situation would have happened regardless of me staying or leaving? Would I still have chosen to stay there if I knew this was destined to happen? To literally see the occurrence first hand, or to get another call from a hospital letting me know my husband had another overdose?

What if, as shitty as the situations were, God, or whoever, whatever, is in charge knew the beauty that could come from me experiencing this? What if this greater plan envisioned what I would do with my hardships, how I could take them, and the impact I could bring to the world because of what happened.

We are all connected, every single one of us. Maybe there are plans out there better than our own. We don't have the birds-eye view to see all of the possibilities to come. To see the ripple effect of a few small or big actions.

My hope is that the ripple effect is good, and that Michael will still be able to make the life-changing impact he wanted to make in this world, that he can still make our son proud.

Whether it's helping someone with their marriage problems, seeking help, pursuing a scary goal, or choosing to take steps towards healthier coping mechanisms, I hope sharing our story can impact someone's life in some shape or form. Maybe yours.

If, at the very least, you can gain a new perspective on love and forgiveness despite hardships.

CHAPTER 11: SPIRITUALITY

Immediately after finding out he died, my spirituality went completely numb. I no longer knew what I believed. I didn't know what to tell my son. I didn't even know if I believed in heaven anymore, or if there was a point to this world. I was emotionless.

I remember his book recommendation, and seeing the ways Michael had grown over the four years of our marriage. Regardless of us being separated and complicated, it blew my mind hearing from an old friend of his that he had asked her how she would feel if he became a believer, and hearing from people he did bible studies with.

Not once did I ever force him to attend services with me while we lived together; I simply offered and would go alone or with a friend. I never held it against him; I simply let him do his thing. I knew God wasn't just found in the services anyway. I never told Michael about the weeks I prayed about the person he was slowly becoming, but to see it coming to fruition was beautiful even if I wasn't ready to receive it and needed more time.

While I might have lost my own faith over time, it felt good knowing he was at least feeling a calling towards a higher power and a relationship with our creator. Truth be told, I'm still figuring out my faith even now, but I have faith we'll reconnect someday. I tell our son how proud Michael is of him and how he's always watching over him. I hope it's true.

I know I have songs come across my station from time to time, and I can just sense that they're different. They feel like they're from him and generally help push me through from time to time or when I just need a good crying session.

Wherever he is, I know he's better. Whatever suffering he had, whatever negativity and anxieties he had rolling through his mind constantly, they're gone now. And for that, I'm thankful. Even if there are still a million thoughts I have of conversations I wish I could be having with him.

CHAPTER 12: MOVING FORWARD

I can forever wish things had gone differently. For days at a time, I would run myself to the ground with scenario after scenario of all the things I could have done differently. *If only I had, what if I had, I shouldn't have,* but all that did was waste time and emotions. No matter how many times I thought up a different scenario in my head, the reality was the same.

I had to start telling myself, *"it is what it is."* As simple and mundane of a statement, it's also a strong one. It's accepting reality, regardless of the other outcome options I would have liked to take instead. I had to have a heart to heart with myself and finally admit that I was a widow, that my son was fatherless, and that my marriage made it to *"til death do us part."*

Not in the way that this was now my identity, but more so that this was now a part of me and my story. For the first few years, I grieved "the father of my child," or "my son's dad." I would say things like "my former husband," not even realizing it was my own form of avoidance. All of these titles put the grieving away from being a wife and away from being a true widow.

I was still a wreck, but I only grieved for my child and not for myself. I didn't truly allow myself to be sad about the opportunities lost, or the chance of a redeemed marriage disappearing overnight. It wasn't until a friend pointed out my wording that I realized what I was doing, and after a wave of more grief, I started to heal more.

And when I say heal, I don't mean suddenly I was no longer emotional, but more so I was able to accept what "it is." That I lost my husband, the father of my child, and someone I loved and cared for dearly despite what the outside world might have seen. If you're reading this book, you're the first person I've shared most of these stories with.

I kept them as my little secrets for almost the last seven years. Not even my closest friends knew about a majority of what I've shared until I wrote this for the public, but it has been healing even with all the tears. Even if it still feels like a dream. It was a story I needed to share, and I hope it's been beneficial.

Over Memorial Day weekend of this year (2021), I completed my first Murph Challenge. If you don't know what that is, it's a CrossFit inspired workout of the day where each person completes a 1-mile run, 100 pull-ups, 200 push-ups, 300 squats, followed by one last 1-mile run, all with a 20lb vest on.

I thought of Michael and how pissed he would be to

see me moping my life away in bed. To see the person he had admired just rotting away her potential. I owed it to myself, my child, and him to do more with my life.

So I pulled out the photo of him completing SERE school for a quick reminder, put on his SFAS recruiting shirt, and went out into the hundred-some degree weather to complete my first challenge.

I wanted to quit so badly. I was feeling lightheaded, I was sweating so bad, and I was feeling very out of shape. I took breaks, I slowed down, I rested in the shade and snacked on Sour Patch kids with water for added energy, so I didn't pass out, but I didn't quit. All I could think about was all of the rigorous training he put himself through. Most of it I didn't even know in-depth about. But I just kept thinking that if he could make it through all of that training, I could finish that challenge.

And I did, in just around an hour and a half time. I share this Murph story because it applies to more than just the workout I did that day. It applies to any challenges put on my plate.

While I've been dealt some not-so-fun cards, so have every single one of us. You can read my story and say how strong or how brave I am, but I guarantee there are areas in your life that I could say the very same to you. We push forward because that is the only option. Any other decision isn't choosing to live, and life is too short not to live it fully.

CLOSING WORDS

While it still breaks my heart, and I can't even begin to tell you how many times I cried writing and rereading this book, I knew I had to write it. I wanted to share the other side of drug abuse while shedding an empathetic light. I wanted to show what can happen when trauma isn't worked through in a healthy manner, and how it can affect those that surround us.

I wanted to share because you and those you love are deserving of healing, of being healthy, happy, and loved. I also wanted to share that every relationship will have its struggles. It's up to you to decide what struggles you're willing to fight for with your significant other.

The grass is rarely ever greener on the other side, and not everyone is willing to put in the work needed to become a better person. It does require patience though, actual change can't just happen overnight, and many of us, unfortunately, lack the patience to see it through.

Life moves on, but the grief never really goes away. I would never have thought in just under five years I could see someone's life change so much. It felt like a blink of an eye writing this, while I know it felt like decades in the hard times.

Sometimes I still feel like I disassociate, like it's all just a dream, but I guess that goes back to my poem of "Maybe Then" (at the end of this book), and I can now say that even writing an entire book and publishing my story still hasn't made it feel real, even with the tears. Even with having to snap myself back to this reality, it still feels like I experienced a dream. Like I'm sharing a dream I had. Except it was a massive chunk within a decade of my life.

My hope is that moving forward, I will get to gain a licensure over the next few years and become a therapist as either an LCSW or a doctor in clinical psychology with a specialization in trauma and substance abuse. Whether that's focused on the military population or not, only time will tell, but it's where I'm feeling the most called towards currently.

I look at the cards that I was dealt in life, and I've always felt like it would be a disservice not to take the hard times and turn them into a call towards success—

finding the beauty in the wreckage, as cliche as it is.

However this book found you, I hope it leaves you with a gained perspective on life. I hope it allows you to forgive those that have done you wrong. Because ultimately, the forgiveness is for you anyway. But most importantly, I hope you live your life to your fullest potential.

I hope you seek the help you need, as needed, and you kick ass in this short life. The world needs every single one of our individual sparks, passions, and successes. Go out and get after yours.

IN HONOR OF MICHAEL:

"And when I turned to face grief,
I saw that it was just love in a heavy coat"
- Shannon Barry

"Mike was a huge part of my life during our 09-10 deployment. Doc was bullet proof. I can't comprehend this. I got out and he went to selection. He was a badass and I am a better person by knowing him. I would tell him how proud I was of the man he was turning out to be. We used to play guitar together on deployment. Most of the rifts I know are ones he taught me.

I'll never forget how he and I were perched up on the side of a mountain pulling overwatch when a sniper missed him by inches. He was a tough guy with lots of love for us. Anytime anyone was under the weather and such, he'd do everything he could for them. He was a great medic and a good friend. The light in his eye brightened and his attitude changed for the better when Christian was born.

Ugh, it hurts....

He had a heart of gold. Quitting wasn't an option for him. He would see things through to the bitter end despite challenge. I miss him."

- R.G.

"Fastest way down a snowy mountain top in Afghanistan? With your medic and his Skedco of course."

- **S.S.**

"Lot of great memories with you man. From fast cars and fast motorcycles, walking up and down the mountains of Afghanistan, no matter what we did the main thing I remember about you is that you were always smiling. So now when I think about you I just picture you smiling at me from heaven and laughing at me every time I do something goofy. Take care of those Angels like you took care of the US soldiers. Love you brother. May you rest peacefully."

- J.L.

"Mike, I've written this so many different times I can't even think of where to start. So I'll start like this, I miss you. I have so many great memories of you but my favorite is that you were a genuinely good person. You honestly cared about us and we all knew it. You were an amazing soldier, and a great friend. You will forever be missed. I look forward to the day when I can tell your son about the man his father was. I love you."

"Mikey worked his ass off. He knew his job and knew it well. I don't think I've ever met a medic I felt as close to. Last deployment, we would sit and BS through the plywood wall but I would always listen to him play Bayside on guitar and I would fall asleep to it every time."

- T.E.

"As I sit here in Afghanistan, I just want to say that you, Christian, and Mike are in my thoughts. Last time I talked to Mike was before I graduated the Q course. My fondest memory of him was when he was role playing when I went through Robin Sage. He snuck me candy and food because he knew I was hurting. He was also a stellar medic as well. I owe a lot of my success at Sage to Mike. In this difficult time, I hope that warmth and comfort finds you and your son."

- E.Y.

"I still remember the day my platoon came back from the JSS. We got back to the COP just before day break and we were all ready for some hot chow. We knew that while we're out on the JSS, for a month, that our security element at the COP had switched out and that we would be seeing new faces. So we're sitting in the DFAC shoveling food in our faces while looking at all the new faces from the MP unit walking through.

I remember like it was yesterday when I looked up and saw this little funny looking muscle bound dude walking through the door. I literally dropped my fork and said "Mike?!" He turned and looked and came over fast as hell to give me a big hug. Literally hadn't seen the kid since high school, 5 years prior, yet here we were on COP Nerkh, Afghanistan together.

My platoon accepted him as one of our own and we all got close. Always in the gym, my platoons hooch, or over at the shop on the COP eating our Naan and playing cards. When I left to come back stateside that was the last time I saw Mike. We messaged back and forth a good bit. We didn't talk a lot after he started SF training. Our last conversation was Dec 29, 2016..."

"...Then one day I jumped on facebook and I had a message telling me that Mike was gone. I reached out to as many as I could in hope that it wasn't true. But it was and I couldn't believe it. The man that I spent so much time with overseas, the man who took care of my guys after hitting an ied to get back to the COP while we finished security and getting the scene cleaned up. I was then making arrangements to escort him home."

- B.L.

"I was new to the Army and unit when we first deployed and before that he took me and my wife out to eat to tell me what to expect with our company and what deployment will be like. Once we were downrange my wife had a brain aneurism and I was sent home. Before I went I had all of our guys sign a flag. He had pulled me aside, I was a complete wreck, pissed upset, and he talked to me for a good while. You know he was there for us always, even when morale was down he was always joking around. We lost a hell of a person."

- J.M.

"He organized a speech downtown at the library. It was for his class, but he did it as an outreach too. He wanted to create an opportunity for people to share their testimonies too, which we did. He and his friend shared their classes, and his was about how people reaching out to him had impacted his faith. He had invited people in from the streets and we had some of the homeless folks come in to join us and got to feed them too. I know he would have been interested in doing more homeless outreach too, he really seemed to care about people and get that message of hope out there.

There were a few times he looked really down. One night about 9 months ago when the lord put him on my heart big time. We hadn't seen him in a while, so J and I kept reaching out to him until he finally reached back. He came out that night and I could tell he was really distressed.

He gave us a class (that was how we got him to come out, since he needed 10 people to talk to) on depression and suicide, and I couldn't help but feel like he was telling us his own story..."

"...Another guy in our ministry, L, had been struggling with the same things, and after the fact, Mike actually encouraged him. He was telling L to keep seeking the Lord and he would give him the encouragement to get through it. So I know Mike was trying to seek the Lord, and as you mentioned, was struggling with a lot of deep, spiritual warfare. But L said he had been considered hurting himself that night, and did not, because we had invited him out. I see that as God giving him more time and being there for him in his time of need."

- C.M.

A NOTE TO CHRISTIAN:

Your dad loved you so much. The way he would light up being around you. His excitement for all of your developmental chapters. How badly I would love for him to be here in person as you grow up. I see so much of your dad in you. I hope that you can read this whenever the time is right and know that we were both so grateful to have you in our lives. I still am. Even through the hardships, you have been such a blessing. I'm looking forward to seeing what you accomplish as the years go by. I love you so much.

- Mom

"MAYBE THEN..."

Maybe then it'll be real, I told myself. Maybe then.

Maybe when the two uniformed men come to officially tell me the news. Maybe then it'll feel real. But I just made dumb army jokes and showed my veteran card on complete accident and felt guilty for laughing and making lame jokes.

Maybe as I sign paper after paper with your name on it and receive military forms with your time and location of death it'll feel real.

Maybe when the service members carry your body off the plane, as ugly tears run down my face yet again and our child asks where daddy is while we're standing on the tarmac. Military personnel surrounding us. Firefighters with the large American flag hanging in the background. Maybe then it'll be real. But that moment passed and it didn't.

Maybe when I see you again for the first time in months and touch your hand in that open casket. That time it'll have to feel real. But it didn't. You just looked like some type of dressed-up military mannequin. It wasn't you.

Maybe when they do the 21 gun salute.
When we're handed the folded flag that carried you home draped across your casket.

How can none of this make it feel real?
How can I carry so many tears yet be so numb?

Maybe when I finally get the investigation report. As I skim through the autopsy readings with the in-depth description of your death and the events leading up to your final breath. How much more real could it get?

But it still wasn't.
Sure tears rolled down my face,
but it wasn't the thing to make it real.

Maybe when we finally visit the gravesite. When we see the gravestone with your name on it. As we eat your favorite stuffed crust pizza, watermelon sour patch kids, and I pour out a beer and bring you one last dip can... maybe then.

But it's been years.
And I'll be honest with you...

Nothing ever felt real.

Not even writing this book.
Even with all of the emotions,
it just felt like reliving a dream.

SFQC STAGES:

For those curious about the different phases of Special Forces I address in this book, Special Forces Qualification Course (SFQC). The order and time frames might change as the years go by, but this was the essentials that are shared on government websites. Some things are excluded and you'll only find out if you're actually in the program yourself.

/ / / / /

Individuals have to first make it through selection, also known as SFAS, a 19 day experience testing mental, physical, and teamwork. They then go to Airborne school if they aren't already Airborne qualified, which means they learn how to jump out of airplanes and parachute down on their own.

Those looking to become an 18D like Michael was complete the special operations combat medics course (SOCM) before beginning anything else in the special operations training. This course lasts 36 weeks, and includes in-class training and interning. After completing SOCM they begin the Special Forces training.

Small-Unit Tactics (SUT) and Survival, Evasion, Resistance, and Escape (SERE) training is the next training phase. SUT is approximately a six-week training of working as a team where individuals are graded by those working alongside them and the instructors. SERE is a three-week training where individuals are taken hostage and put through different interrogation tactics simulating being a prisoner of war, followed by psychological evaluations.

The next phase is based on the specialty, so for 18D, they start working in different settings learning specialty medical skills. This is approximately 14-week medical sergeant focus.

The final phases include Robin Sage and language school. Robin sage is a five-week long training with the team practicing special operations tactics, and language school is an 18 to 24-week training where they are fully submerged in learning a new language and the culture of that area.

After completing these phases, individuals will be pinned their Oppresso De Libre ("Free the Oppressed") pin and officially earn their green beret.

RESOURCES:

In relation to this book, I wanted to put together a handful of resources that may be beneficial. These are all mental health or military-related. I can't guarantee the websites, emails, or phone numbers will always be valid, but all links and data are correct at the time of publication. These are all chosen by me. I get nothing from mentioning any companies and references below. I have simply followed or been involved in them and appreciate the work and successes I've seen so far.

/ / / / /

MENTAL HEALTH AMERICA SCREENING
https://screening.mhanational.org/
This website offers free testing for mental health-related areas like anxiety, depression, addiction, PTSD, etc. In addition to testing, they have DIY tools and resources. While it isn't used for a diagnosis, it can help to get a general idea before seeing a provider.

SUBSTANCE ABUSE AND MENTAL HEALTH

https://www.samhsa.gov/

1-800-662-HELP (4357) Or 1-800-487-4889

While I've never used this site or the hotline, it's one that's generally shared during mental health awareness month or with veteran suicide awareness, etc. They offer a hotline and different resources for finding local support groups, treatment facilities, and communities based on the needs of the caller.

TALKSPACE

https://www.talkspace.com/

I've used both Betterhelp and Talkspace but personally had a better experience with Talkspace. While everyone's needs are different, I personally enjoyed using these platforms rather than the traditional form of therapy sessions because I was able to text in or send a voice message to my therapist as I was feeling the emotions rather than trying to jot them down to save for my next appointment when the feelings and thoughts weren't so fresh. It allowed me to quickly pick up on my own patterns and is something I will still get on from time to time when I'm dealing with struggles. Everyone is different though. Some may benefit more from seeing a regular provider in person. This is also limited if you are looking towards a medication route to help as they are unable to prescribe anything.

WE DEFY FOUNDATION

https://www.wedefyfoundation.org/
This is the company that indirectly helped me push through a massive depression. Their Veteran's Day video found on Facebook and Youtube, "This is Normal," hit me so hard that I knew it was time to do something about my own situation. They focus on helping disabled combat veterans by providing them with new coping methods through martial arts - particularly Brazilian Jiu-Jitsu.

PB ABBATE

https://www.pbabbate.org/
There are many veteran-based communities, but this has been hands down the most diverse and focused on finding a true life outside of the military that I've personally come across over the years. They have set up different clubs and chapters around the U.S. in areas like book club, fight club, writers club, surfing, etc.

HEROIC HEARTS PROJECT

https://www.heroicheartsproject.org/

They are sharing alternative ways of healing through ayahuasca and other psychedelic therapies. This company takes veterans on a retreat in places like Peru and Jamaica to work through a spiritual/holistic healing experience.

DEAD RECKONING COLLECTIVE

https://deadreckoningco.com/

This is a Veteran owned print publication company that also offers writing workshops. While I chose to self-publish and have not worked with them directly, I have personally found so much healing from writing my story, and I know many others can as well. I love that their focus is on publishing for veterans and helping them with writing.

SOFLETE TRAINING

https://soflete.com/

Nutrition and getting the body moving are key factors that can influence our minds. When we aren't treating our body well, our mind goes with it. SOFLETE has a monthly app membership where you can receive meal ideas, daily workouts, and a way to track everything. I love that they also focus on cognitive skills, something easily forgotten about for many of us. Even if you don't want to do the app, their social media always has a great workout available.

EMDR INTERNATIONAL ASSOCIATION
https://www.emdria.org/
EMDR is Eye Movement Desensitization and Reprocessing. It's a method of therapy that has helped a number of people, and I wanted to use it as an additional resource for finding providers near you or for training opportunities. I've personally never tried it but have heard it's been beneficial.

www.ingramcontent.com/pod-product-compliance
Lightning Source LLC
Chambersburg PA
CBHW042126100526
44587CB00026B/4185